Beyond the Bard

 W9-DCG-462

Related Titles

Opening Doors, Opening Opportunities: Family Literacy in an Urban Community
Jeanne R. Paratore
ISBN: 0-205-27492-7

You Never Asked Me to Read: Useful Assessment of Reading and Writing Problems
Jay Simmons
ISBN: 0-205-28854-5

Writers' Workshop: Reflections of Elementary and Middle School Teachers
Bobbie A. Solley (Editor)
ISBN: 0-205-29015-9

Literacy Strategies Across the Subject Areas: Process-Oriented Blackline Masters for the K–12 Classroom
Karen D. Wood
ISBN: 0-205-32658-7

Promoting Literacy in Grades 4–9: A Handbook for Teachers and Administrators
Karen D. Wood and Thomas S. Dickinson (Editors)
ISBN: 0-205-28314-4

For more information or to purchase a book, please call 1-800-278-3525.

Beyond the Bard

Fifty Plays for Use
in the English Classroom

Joshua Rutsky

Hoover High School
Hoover, Alabama

Allyn and Bacon
Boston ▪ London ▪ Toronto ▪ Sydney ▪ Tokyo ▪ Singapore

Series editor: Arnis E. Burvikovs
Series editorial assistant: Patrice Mailloux
Marketing manager: Stephen Smith

Copyright © 2001 by Allyn & Bacon
A Pearson Education Company
Needham Heights, MA 02494

Internet: www.abacon.com

All rights reserved. No part of the material protected by this copyright notice may be reproduced or utilized in any form or by any means, electronic or mechanical, including photocopying, recording, or by any information storage and retrieval system, without written permission from the copyright owner.

Between the time Web site information is gathered and then published, it is not unusual for some sites to have closed. Also, the transcription of URLs can result in unintended typographical errors. The publisher would appreciate notification where these occur so that they may be corrected in subsequent editions. Thank you.

Library of Congress Cataloging-in-Publication Data

Rutsky, Joshua.
    Beyond the bard : fifty plays for use in the English classroom / Joshua Rutsky.
        p. cm.
    Includes indexes.
    ISBN 0-205-30809-0
    1. Drama—Stories, plots, etc.   I. Title.
PN6112.5 .R88 2001
809.2—dc21

                                                                00-045392

Printed in the United States of America

10   9   8   7   6   5   4   3   2   1   04   03   02   01   00

To Becki, who made this happen

CONTENTS

PREFACE

Beyond the Bard began as part of a project for a graduate course. The more teachers I talked to, the clearer it became that there is little exposure to drama in teachers' undergraduate and graduate training. Literature classes are required for aspiring English teachers, but those classes usually focus on novels and poetry. Unless the teachers-to-be are involved in a college drama group or some similar activity, the odds are that they will have a limited knowledge of the wide range of plays that have been published in the last five hundred years.

This struck me as a shame, particularly because drama as a teaching tool makes perfect sense to me. After all, isn't teaching very similar to acting? We perform for our audience, the students, hopefully conveying our message through tone, gesture, and a variety of tricks to hold their attention. If we perform in our classrooms, why not incorporate that performance experience into our teaching?

It also seems logical to use drama as a way of containing and channeling a particularly energetic class. A student who is too loud or insists on clowning in class is often looking for attention. Drama provides a way to give these students the attention they crave while still keeping control and focus in your classroom. Instead of confronting a student head-on about a behavioral problem, a teacher can use drama to form a cooperative relationship, encouraging success in an area where the student has natural talent.

The goal of this text is to help you, the teacher, quickly and easily find a play that will let you take advantage of the benefits of drama in the classroom. You can browse through the reviews alphabetically, or you can search for a play with a specific theme by using the indexes at the back of this book. Since the plays reviewed date from the Renaissance to the present, there are options here for every grade level and curriculum. Each review is designed to help you efficiently locate the information that you need. In addition to publication date, length and setting, number of lead roles, and a plot summary, each review contains a list of suggestions for building connections between the play and a lesson plan. The primary themes of each play are outlined as well, so that you can link it to your curriculum as either a companion piece to a particular text or as part of a year-long investigation of a theme.

A play may appear to be an ideal thematic match for a particular unit, but a good teacher knows that the content must be in a vehicle suitable for his or her classroom. Unfortunately, that can mean a painstaking two- or three-hour reading of the text during valuable preparation time, in search of potentially objectionable material. Each review in this book, however, provides a summary of language, action, and thematic material that might be considered inappropriate. This allows a teacher to quickly rule out a play that fails to meet their school's standards.

Few teachers enjoy using another teacher's detailed lesson plan in their own classroom. Like the students they teach, teachers are all different, each with his or her own style. For the teacher who is in a hurry, but still wants enough flexibility to put his or her own creative ideas into a lesson or assignment, the "Unit Bull's-eye" evaluation exercise shown in Appendix B is the answer. It provides a complete sequence of ready-to-use exercises for evaluation and expansion in a drama-based unit, and it can be easily adapted for use in novel- or poetry-based units, as well.

With reviews, planning ideas, and ready-to-use activities, *Beyond the Bard* is designed to give you the help you need to bring drama into your classroom.

Acknowledgments

No task as large as writing a book can be achieved without the help of others. I'd like to thank all of those who helped bring this project to fruition, including Joe Strzepek at the University of Virginia's Curry School of Education, who first saw potential in this work; Margo Figgins, Susan Minsk, Diane Martin, Elma Tuohy, Robert Cooper, and Dorothy Vasquez-Levy, who all made invaluable contributions to my development as an English teacher; Charles Ellis, who gave me a start in drama, and Evy Gildrie-Voyles, who taught me to truly love it; my wife, Rebecca, who kept my writing honest and made sure I met deadlines; my family, who supported my efforts and engaged in countless discussions of plays they'd never encountered before; my closest consultant, M. B. Ampers, who was happy to listen to my complaints over meals; and, of course, the students in Mr. Rutsky's Neighborhood at Albemarle High School in Charlottesville, Virginia; Indian Springs School in Indian Springs, Alabama; and Hoover High School in Hoover, Alabama, who will someday change the world in the way that they change my life daily.

INTRODUCTION

It was the first day of tenth-grade English class, and Mrs. Tuohy was distributing the textbooks for the semester. The stacks in front of us grew one by one as she passed out the clean copies—Joyce, Dickens, a copy of *The Norton Introduction to Poetry*. And then it happened.

I suppose we all knew it was coming; it happens to every American student at one point or another in their high school lives. For many of us, it was a yearly challenge, a preview of the fun we'd have with tax forms in the future. I'm speaking, of course, of our annual installment of Shakespeare. Welcomed by students with the enthusiasm generally reserved for a trip to the dentist, the Shakespeare play was as much a part of our English classes as paragraph structure lectures or vocabulary ditto sheets. The first encounter, *Romeo and Juliet*, took place in eighth grade, followed by *The Merchant of Venice* in ninth. This year would yield a bumper crop—both *Macbeth* and *King Lear* were on the reading list. The next year, *Hamlet* would be the work of choice, and for the brave senior, *Othello*. The Shakespeare of the Year was a fixture we expected, and occasionally we even enjoyed reading the plays. I left high school, however, with a very narrow understanding of drama. My only experiences with plays were my encounters with Shakespeare, a quick read of Sophocles' *Oedipus Rex* in Advanced Placement English, and a small role in a musical during my senior year.

I didn't know I was missing anything until I got to college, took a class in drama, and discovered a wide world of vibrant stories, told in a language I could understand without referring to a glossary, and spoken in normal cadences, not iambic pentameter. What a change to go from *Othello* to *Death and the King's Horseman* or from *Hamlet* to *Waiting for Godot*! The characters, plots, settings, language, staging—they opened up possibilities for literature I had never before considered. In my freshman year at Oberlin, I saw a brilliant production of the short opera *Sister Angelica* that really drove home this new freedom. The script calls for the Virgin Mary to appear to Sister Angelica at the close of the opera, a vision come to forgive her for taking poison in a fit of despair. Instead of using an actress to play the Virgin (a nonspeaking role), and having her appear from a cloud of fog, the director instead had a picture of the Madonna and Child slowly brought into focus against the white backdrop. The effect was outstanding; the director found a way to re-create for the audience what was meant to occur in a character's *mind*.

The creativity I saw on stage that night changed my way of thinking about drama. For the first time, I really believed that I could *interact* with the texts I read; my choices, my readings of characters' tones, and the things I envisioned them doing as they spoke all affected the way the action unfolded on stage. I was suddenly being encouraged by my professors to explore, expand, and experiment. And I wondered as I left the class why I had never been given the same opportunities by my high school teachers.

I was still wondering that four years later, when I returned to Alabama and to my old high school, Indian Springs, as a first-time teacher. The syllabus that had been assembled for the eleventh-grade course I was teaching contained the same play I had encountered when I was a junior—*Hamlet. Waiting for Godot* had been added to the reading list, small comfort for the students who would find it harder to understand than sixteenth-century English. I was disappointed, both as a teacher and as a student, by the absence of drama in the curriculum. Teachers widely acknowledge that getting students actively involved in the discussion of a text is preferable to delivering straight lectures to bored listeners. We try to take our students to the theater so that they can experience drama in performance, because we know that seeing a story take shape in front of us is somehow more vivid, more lively, more engaging than simply reading a book. Yet for some reason, we regularly fail to take advantage of the most flexible, participatory form of text readily available in our classrooms. Why?

The Benefits of Drama

It doesn't have to be this way. Many teachers have successfully incorporated drama into the classroom, and not just the same old standbys. These teachers know that there's something to be gained from using plays instead of, or as complements to, novels and poetry—accessibility. In *An Unquiet Pedagogy,* Eleanor Kutz and Hephzibah Roskelly attest to the value of the form:

> Dramatic literature offers unique opportunities for groups to work productively, since drama is created as a collaborative effort among actors, writer, director, stage designer, and audience. In fact, one of the real problems in interpreting drama—envisioning its performance—is circumvented by group work where group members can take on those roles. Groups can . . . "block" the movements of the actors on stage by interpreting characters' motivations in a scene . . . read scenes aloud, prepare roles, do staged readings. . . . They can rewrite scenes. . . . In doing this work, the group re-creates the play: the relationship between actor and character, between audience and writer, between production and interpretation. . . . (261)

Kutz and Roskelly are absolutely right. I believe that drama is the most accessible form of literature, one centered in active, not passive, experiences. When a play is read or performed, it is happening. When a student reads a novel, the characters speak through the voice of the narrator, and the action is recollected, recounted—in the past. Drama allows the teacher to bring the students into the action, rather than merely discussing it. Plays can be walked through, interpreted, and manipulated far more easily than novels, and that gives us the opportunity to engage students with the text in new and exciting ways.

If plays are so terrific, why aren't they in wide use in classrooms? I've spent the last few years asking that question, and the answers I've gotten from fellow teachers have been enlightening. Frequently, I was told that the lack of plays on the syllabus was a reflection of the teacher's own education; having rarely encountered drama as a student, he or she was uncomfortable teaching it extensively. The inclusion of Shakespeare became the teacher's gesture to the genre, and they stuck with the major plays because they were the familiar stories that they knew how to teach. There are plenty of teaching aids available for *Macbeth*, for example; several versions of the play are available on videotape, and books of criticism abound. A complete study edition is available for any of Shakespeare's major works, containing all the interpretive notes and critical essays a teacher might need to prepare for a class. Using these aids certainly doesn't make one a bad teacher; they provide valuable information in a concise form, well suited for a committed teacher's busy schedule. With the provided notes, teachers can make drama discussions interesting and enlightening, even if they themselves aren't well versed in the genre. Such teachers may ask the students to read a few scenes from their seats, and they are likely to discuss the development of the genre, but they aren't comfortable enough with drama to wade in and make it an *experience* rather than a simple text.

Other teachers have more experience with drama and are capable of enlivening a traditional Shakespeare class with alternative language, performance choice discussions, role-playing, scene walkthroughs, and other exercises. They are comfortable leading the class through participatory exercises and aren't afraid of trading "thees" and "thous" with their students. These are teachers like the one who, when asked why Shakespeare was the only drama on his syllabus, replied, "I'd love to do more, but I really don't know enough plays to pick one appropriate to my class this semester." This teacher was not undereducated; he was taking evening classes with me at the University of Virginia when we spoke, and I was continually impressed by his experience and skill. Like many other teachers, he had read or seen some of the "great dramas" but was unfamiliar with anything beyond the canon traditionally found in high school classrooms and in introductory college courses. Given time, he could find a suitable play to include in his curriculum, but time is short for most of us. If it takes a reader even two hours to read a full-length play, reviewing ten plays to choose a suitable one becomes a three-day activity! Without guidelines to narrow the search, this time commitment makes adding new plays to the syllabus a difficult task.

Unfortunately, few resources are available to provide teachers with the information they need to select a play they have not seen and incorporate it successfully into their course plan. What few compendiums are available are usually highly specific, focusing on a period (such as the nineteenth century) or a subdivision of the genre (e.g., "experimental" theater or female playwrights). They rarely provide plot summaries or any other condensed information about the plays, and the teacher must read and digest the work before deciding if it is suitable.

This problem has been dealt with in other genres through the creation of teachers' guide books—collections of outlines and teaching suggestions designed to make the educator's life a little easier. Books such as *500 Great Books by Women* (1994) offer the teacher short sketches of a range of novels, indexed in several ways to provide maximum utility. This book is intended to offer the same options for the use of plays in your classroom.

What You'll Find Inside

In the following pages, you'll find a variety of plays selected from across the centuries. There are traditional favorites, such as plays by Shaw, Goldsmith, and Ibsen, and works by less familiar playwrights, such as Centlivre, Dürrenmatt, and Ives. You'll even find one of Shakespeare's most frequently performed but infrequently taught plays. Each of the reviews provides key information on the work in question as well. Want to find a play with enough parts for the entire class? Or one that has a female lead for each woman in your class? You'll find a list of characters, along with play length, date of publication, and setting, grouped at the beginning of each review.

A quick one- or two-paragraph synopsis of the play's action is followed by an entry listing the major themes addressed by the playwright. Use these categories to quickly locate a play that fits into your lesson plan, either thematically or through story connections. Building bridges between text and play is also simplified by the inclusion of a "connections and suggestions" paragraph. Each play has several ideas for classroom integration, as well as the names of other plays or novels that complement the work. Some ideas are more detailed than others, but all are immediately usable in your classroom.

Finally, and perhaps most important, two final notes round out each entry in this collection. The "red flags" section provides you with a list of potentially objectionable material within the play in question—something you should know *before* you find yourself face-to-face with it in the classroom. With this resource, you can quickly eliminate material unsuitable for your students without reading the entire play. The last line of each entry offers a suggested minimum age for appreciation of the play, so that you don't accidentally give your eighth graders *Waiting for Godot* or *Manfred*. Comprehensive indexes by period and by subject matter are included at the end of the book to allow quick identification of the plays most suitable for your situation.

Some Suggestions for Starting Out

Of course, we can't just drop a play into our students' laps and ask them to run with it. Although drama can be liberating and extremely accessible, if we intend to make the most of it, we need to be prepared to help students make the transition from distanced reader to active participant and interpreter. To get students comfortable enough to take charge of the text and make it their own, we need to convince them that it is safe to experiment, to rethink, and to act out. While teaching, and in my visits to other teachers' classrooms in both Alabama and Virginia, I've used a variety of activities to help students break through their self-consciousness and self-censoring, some written and some requiring active participation.

Improvisation

One technique I have found particularly effective in classrooms as an introduction to drama study is improvisational comedy work. Simple improv games get students out of their seats, get them thinking quickly, and make them place themselves in other people's shoes—make them play the "believing game." In one game, Freeze Chain, two students start by acting out a scene. At any time, another student can say, "Freeze!" and the two actors stop immediately. The outsider then taps one of the two on the shoulder, assumes his or her frozen position, and then continues the action in her or his own way, perhaps changing the scene's direction, setting, or characters entirely. I have found such games extremely successful, even in classes filled with reluctant students. First, Freeze Chain allows students to do "nonschool" things for a while, and that always seems appealing to a class stuck in lectures for most of the day. Second, acting out is encouraged in improv work, and students get a chance to cut loose. Many of the students who might be considered behavior problems or troublemakers—the sarcastic kid at the back of the room or the "low achiever"—have excellent mocking or verbal skills but rarely get a chance to shine in a traditional lecture-discussion model English class. These students may well excel in improv, which requires a willingness to perform and a quick wit.

One of my students, John, was a serious introvert, speaking up in class only to land a quick jab of wit or a sarcastic comment about the discussion (or occasionally my personal habits). He wouldn't answer questions, wouldn't participate in the discussions, and was producing the absolute minimum amount of work possible. When I started working with improv as an after-school activity, I asked John to come and try out for the group. He laughed at me at first and wanted to know why I thought he'd want to do something geeky like that. Geeky or no, he still showed up for the group tryout, "just to watch." Soon he found himself surrounded by people cutting loose and not worrying about how they looked to each other, trading jokes and getting laughs. Suddenly—I think it was during a freeze chain, actually, that he first "tagged in"—John was out there, playing the perfect straight man. He was very, very good, and it showed.

By the end of the tryout, John was eager to find out when we would practice. By the end of the year, the former introvert was performing in the school's spring musical and was cast the next year in the fall play as well. His classwork, formerly acceptable, began to improve tremendously as he started to find his own style of communicating. Obviously, not every student is going to find drama as liberating as John did, but I firmly believe that the practice gained in self-expression can only improve a student's sense of voice, and that the creative freedom of the exercises encourages students to take chances and experiment in their writing.

Macbeth is a staple of the senior English curriculum but often a difficult climb for students lagging behind the pack with their reading skills. Shakespeare seems distant even to strong young readers; Michael was ready to throw in the towel for the year when he heard we were about to start in on it. "Geez, Mr. Rutsky," he said in one of the heaviest Brooklyn accents ever to make it to the Southeast, "I oughta just go back to alternative school, 'cause I'm never gonna figure that junk out." While Michael's actual word choice was a bit more colorful than "junk," you get the idea—he was intimidated by Shakespeare and ready to give up before he gave himself a chance. Teaching *Macbeth* in the traditional way would have been fine for three-quarters of Michael's class, but not for him.

Instead of taking the more common, direct approach—reading the play act by act, taking tests after each act to assess comprehension, and then taking a unit test on the entire work—our class approached *Macbeth* as a drama to be read aloud and performed. We talked about motivation, character development, and how the scenes build tension toward a series of climaxes. We watched Akira Kurosawa's film *Throne of Blood,* a Japanese version of *Macbeth,* to decide if the story is still effective presented in a different cultural package. Most important, we *acted.* Scene performance was required; students memorized at least twenty lines and, in groups of two, three, and four, performed either live or on videotape before the class.

The combination of group reading as introduction and acting work as reinforcement made all the difference for Michael. Early on, as we talked about Macbeth's ambition and his growing ruthlessness, Michael began to show a real interest in reading the part of Macbeth. When I asked him why he was suddenly volunteering to read so often, he said, "I like this character. He's kinda like a wiseguy, y'know? He don't take nothing from no one, and if you get in his way, *pffft!* You're through!"

Obviously, Michael didn't understand *Macbeth* as well as I'd have liked. It took a couple of weeks to get him to recognize that Macbeth is aware of how evil he has become and that his conscience torments him. He probably never entirely understood the use of imagery in the play. He did, however, engage with the material. How do I know? Because a week later, I was eating lunch with some of the other teachers who work in my part of the school. One, the teacher in charge of our school's intensive supervision program (that's administrative code for in-school suspension), told me that she had a student from another senior English class who was having trouble understanding *Macbeth.* Michael was also in intensive supervision that day, and when he heard the teacher trying to explain the play to the young man with no success, he poked his head around the corner of the cubicle. "Hey, I can explain that to him," he said. "If there's one thing I've learned real good this year, it's *Macbeth.*" Michael may not have mastered the text, but he learned it well enough that he was confident about reteaching it.

Another student of mine, Kelly, illustrates the kind of person for whom classroom drama is ideal. During the first week of classes in 1997, Kelly got me to throw her out of my class. She was a senior but told me that she had no intention of staying in school any longer than the law made her. Kelly had a reputation for disruption, but I was in my first year of teaching at her school, and I had no idea how often she had been in and out of the principal's office over the past three years.

Our troubles started quickly, on the second day our class met. After asking repeatedly for Kelly and two of her friends to stop talking to one another, I decided to lay down the law. I told Kelly to move to another corner of the classroom, sent one of the other two to a third place, and turned to resume the class. Kelly didn't move. She sat there sullenly but defiantly, staring straight ahead at the blackboard. "Kelly," I said, after waiting a moment, "I asked you to move, please."

Nothing.

I knew that there was nothing I could do. I had to establish authority again, but I had let myself get into the kind of confrontation that can destroy a teacher–student relationship for the rest of the year. I knelt down by Kelly and quietly said to her, "Look, Kelly, I don't want to send you to the office, but you're not giving me a choice. If you don't move, I'll have to write you up."

"You're making a big deal out of nothing!"

"No," I sighed, walking back to my desk. "*You* made a big deal out of nothing. Take this to the office." I handed her her first referral form of the year. It wouldn't be her last, not by a long shot, but it would be the only one she received from me that year.

Kelly didn't come back to the class for the next few days. I went to the principal to ask about her, wanting to know if there was a history behind what I had seen. After all, it seemed like a strange incident to get yourself in trouble over. The principal told me that Kelly's troubles hadn't ended at the classroom door; she had lost her temper while meeting with the assistant principal when he gave her detention, and she had stormed out, earning herself a three-day suspension. "She's a hard case," he said. "She won't accept instructions from anyone. She's ridiculously stubborn and has all sorts of problems. You wouldn't believe her life outside the school, either." Kelly, I learned, was the youngest of a large family whose children largely had to fend for themselves. She was not expected to finish the year at the school.

When Kelly came back to class the next week, we began to negotiate a settlement of sorts. I explained to her that I didn't know her and that I wouldn't look in her file; I wanted her to make her own impression on me, just like all my other students. I told her I intended to take her seriously, but that if she was going to disrupt my class continuously, she'd make that difficult. Kelly was skeptical, but she kept coming to class, and if she wasn't participating, she wasn't nearly as distracting either.

One of the best moments I can remember as a teacher was watching Kelly suddenly explode into life as a student when we started a unit on *Macbeth*. We had just read over the first scene of the play, and I had talked for a while about how the stage would have looked in Shakespeare's day. As eyes were beginning to glaze over, I slammed down my textbook on the desk, making everyone jump. "Move those desks! We've got a production to put on!" The kids stared for a moment as I started hauling desks from the middle of the room to the sides, then joined in. Soon we had our "stage" cleared, and I asked, "Now who wants to play a witch?"

There was silence for a moment, and then, to my surprise and pleasure, Kelly stood up with her book. "I'll be the first witch," she said, "but I want to play Lady Macbeth later."

Kelly took charge for the rest of the day. I got two more volunteers to read the other two parts, but even before I could critique the first reading of the scene, Kelly was telling her partners on stage that they weren't acting like witches. "Besides, if we're talking to each other we should look at each other. And it says we enter and we didn't." She herded the other two into the hall before I could get a word out and then reached in to flick the light switch on and off. "Lightning, Mr. Rutsky," she explained as she and the others came back into the room. At the end of the day, she asked if she could bring in a Halloween witch costume and wear it for the next witch scene.

I'd like to claim credit for some magical conversions as a result of my teaching methods, but I can't. Michael finished his year back in alternative school, and Kelly dropped out early in the second semester. I can, however, say that both students were engaged and learning in my class, whatever problems they faced elsewhere, and I attribute their involvement to the use of drama as a teaching tool. Kelly is just the sort of student for whom drama can really make the difference. She's too active for a normal classroom, and by the end of her first two block-schedule classes she has spent so much energy trying to stay still and "behave" that her temper is shot. She needs a chance to move around and act out, to be praised for taking control and for making a scene. On the stage, she's not causing a disruption—she's at the top of the class, a student with more experience and confidence in being in the public eye than her peers. Kelly is like many of our most disruptive students; she's been designated a problem and is accustomed to the label. She wants attention, from us and from her peers, but the only way she's been successful in getting it has been through forced confrontation.

Erving Goffman pointed out how much we all act on a daily basis in his landmark book, *The Presentation of Self in Everyday Life*. Perhaps we would do well to think of "difficult" students as actors, ones who work particularly hard to perfect their roles as rebel, clown, or even individual. We respect such behavior in professionals. I suggest that viewing these students as budding actors makes it much easier to accept them as they are and to find ways to integrate them into our classes. Once out of the classroom, Kelly will find a job that satisfies her. Most of our students do. Our job is not to change her into our image of a well-behaved citizen but to *teach* her literature and writing skills. Drama let me do that for Kelly and for other so-called difficult students. Improvisation is a natural skill for them; they've practiced it for years without knowing it.

Finally, improv is a good way to get students to think about how actors convey information to their audiences. Students who have practice in improv games learn that facial expression and tone are as important to making meaning as the script and are thus more comfortable taking on roles in dramatic readings of scenes. Building from improv games to play readings and interpretation gives students an opportunity to familiarize themselves with acting in front of their peers as well; once everyone in the class has acted silly, students are much less afraid of embarrassing themselves and more willing to try out a role.

Improv is a good way to open up the class, but you may need other activities to turn to in order to bring the class back to a particular play. I've tried a number of these, some of which worked well and some of which were near disasters. I am particularly fond of three activities, however, that have consistently produced good results: replaying, rewriting, and extending.

Replaying

Replaying activities focus on particular scenes of a play and the opportunities for interpretation within them. Students take parts and do read-throughs in small groups and then discuss the performance choices they want to make for that scene. Will they play a character as honest or sarcastic, as emotional or calm? What does the set look like? Are there props on stage? Do they get used? I ask my students to choose a scene they can perform in at least two different ways and to explain the differences in the performances and why they would choose one interpretation over the other. This exercise also gives students a sense of "ownership" of their reading. Once the initial fear of "changing the play" is conquered, students can be much freer (and much more creative) in their interpretations.

This exercise worked out nicely in my class when we were working on *Waiting for Godot*. Here is a play that has four main characters but with little to describe them outside the text itself, and the only set is an empty road with a small tree beside it. The dialogue takes place with few stage directions, particularly during the longer speeches. At first, my eleventh-grade class was confused—understandably—by the lack of apparent action in the play. "It's *boring*, Mr. Rutsky. Nothing happens! I don't understand what's going on." I really couldn't argue with them; I found reading *Godot* a dull task the first time through, and I really didn't understand much of what was happening either. Turning to writing exercises was obviously out, because they are comprehension based. I decided that we had to try something completely different, or the unit would be a total loss.

The next day, I split the class into two groups and asked each group to sit down for the rest of the period and read the first act to each other. Each group was told to think about how the characters would move and how they would speak and to choose people from the group to act out their interpretation of the script. The students went to work, obviously skeptical. They didn't seem to see how this was going to affect their understanding of the text.

We did the read-through the next day, and it was pretty bad. The readings were wooden, without emotion or inflection, and the students reading the parts generally stood still, holding the script, until the stage directions called for them to move. Even then, the stage direction sometimes took them by surprise, and they weren't where they needed to be for the next line. The problem was that neither group had really *interpreted* the scene. They had read it without trying to act it, and the poor result was obvious to each group as the other read.

When we sat down to talk about the scenes, I pointed out to the class that reading the play was not the same as acting the play. Words on paper have no audible inflection, and we have to depend on context clues to provide the emotional sense of the situation. Words spoken without inflection, however, seem unnatural and actually hinder communication. Once we agreed that reading and acting were different things, we started working on ways to improve the scenes. I pressed particularly hard regarding the difference between reading and interpretation. First, I asked what the groups could do to improve their performances. Movement, they suggested, was very important. Real people don't stand woodenly around while they're talking; they move, wave their hands, sit, toy with shoelaces, and generally look alive.

"Good," I replied, "But how do we decide what the characters are going to do?"

"Stage directions?"

"Stage directions help," I answered, "but do authors put in stage directions for every move the character makes?"

"No, that'd be too hard for the actor to remember."

"So who decides what the actor does when he or she doesn't have a specific stage direction?"

Tentatively—"The actor?"

"Absolutely! The actor has to behave like the character *even when he or she isn't given specific instructions on how to do so!* And when you act in a certain way because you think it's appropriate to the part, that's an interpretation."

This led us to a discussion of interpretation and how directors make performance choices. The next day, we split into new groups and tried the same exercise. The new scenes were markedly better—the students had realized the importance of their own part in the production and tried to contribute to the scene instead of just reading the script. Because they had to think about the text, they also helped themselves unravel the plot. (Of course, the two readings of each scene didn't hurt, either.)

Rewriting

I was able to convince my students that they were allowed to fill in the margins of the text, so to speak, with movement and inflection choices. Although this was a good start toward a willingness to "own" the text, it wasn't enough to convince them that they were equal partners in the reading-acting-reacting process. Rewriting exercises are also meant to increase students' willingness to "mess with the text," to challenge the author's vision or reinterpret it into their own world. In such an exercise, students are asked to take a portion of a larger work—a scene from a play, a chapter of a book, several stanzas of a poem—and alter the language and/or the setting through editing and revision.

Again, the primary benefit of this sort of exercise is to increase students' confidence in their writing skills. Because the activity is focused, there are clear boundaries to guide the student, and there is less risk for the student because the material to rewrite is fixed. Creativity, however, is still encouraged, and individuals can take the revision as far as they choose. Writers who lack confidence can do a partial rewrite exercise, such as producing a modern-language version of an older play. This has the added benefit of creating a study aid that can be distributed to other students, and it reinforces comprehension of the material for the rewriter. It also helps get students in the habit of looking up words they don't understand because they can't produce an accurate rewrite without understanding the vocabulary involved.

Although this exercise is obviously most useful in working with Shakespeare or pre-nineteenth-century authors, students can benefit from transforming modern plays as well. How about asking students to rewrite an act into Shakespearean prose? Or asking them to move a scene from *Waiting for Godot* to the early West? What would be different? What would be the same? Why? One of the best assignments I've received from a student was a rewriting of a love scene from a modern play into morality play form. It showed mastery of both genres and a generous amount of creativity as well!

Extending

Finally, extending exercises ask students to take a part of a play and build on it, to create a fuller world for a character or to prolong a scene. Stage time is rarely linear for all the characters in a play; some take part in the entire drama, while others are onstage for only a few lines. An extension exercise might ask students to invent action and dialogue for their characters during the times the author isn't providing them with lines and directions. What are the characters (not the actors!) saying offstage between their appearances? Do they go home to talk to husbands and wives about their day? Buy a cappuccino at a local coffee bar? (Tom Stoppard's play *Rosencrantz and Guildenstern Are Dead* is the most famous example of this type of extension.) Inventing these dialogues and scenes allows students to see themselves as equals of the author of the original play, and that conveys authority. With a sense of authority comes increased confidence and willingness to speak out in discussions and make critical interpretations of the play.

Extension exercises such as these can be difficult, but they are rewarding. Teachers, however, may wish to step students up to more complicated assignments by asking them to start with simpler extensions. One early assignment in my class each year is to extend one of the stories we study, such as *Beowulf* or the Arthurian legends, by adding either a sequel or prequel story for one of the characters. In a prequel, students create a story explaining how a character (e.g., Beowulf, Guinevere, or the Green Knight) comes to be where he or she is at the start of the story. What is Beowulf like as a child? What was the Green Knight doing the year before he arrives and issues his challenge to Arthur's court? I usually allow students to write these prequels in their own style, but I offer extra credit to ambitious writers who try to mimic the original author's style. Sequels are similar extension exercises, but the writer creates an adventure that takes place after the events in the original story, not before. In both cases, however, the stories created must logically cohere—characters can't die if they appear later in the original story, for example.

Again, the point of such exercises is improving students' confidence in their writing, as well as increasing their comprehension of the core materials. The key to all of these exercises, however, is the willingness of the teacher and the students to commit to the believing game. If the teacher can't convince students that the classroom is a safe space for exploration and acting, for theorizing and for writing, then these exercises will almost certainly fail. The teacher who is convincing, however, can open up a new world of opportunities for the students to explore.

In the pages that follow, you'll find the results of several years of reading and viewing research. The fifty plays I've chosen to review are only a few of the hundreds I've pored over, but each one can enhance a unit or open a new door for discussion. Drama in the classroom is a very potent teaching tool, and properly employed it can bring students into the midst of the action. If active learning is our goal, then we should take advantage of effective methods of achieving that goal and use all the materials at our disposal. As Shakespeare said, "All the world's a stage"; but it doesn't have to be his stage alone.

References

Bauermeister, E., J. Larsen, and H. Smith. *Five Hundred Great Books by Women: A Reader's Guide.* New York: Penguin, 1994.

Goffman, Erving. *The Presentation of Self in Everyday Life.* New York: Doubleday, 1959.

Kutz, Eleanor, and Hephzibah Roskelly. *An Unquiet Pedagogy.* Portsmouth, NH: Boynton/Cook, 1991.

The Reviews

The Amen Corner

1968

James Baldwin

Characters: 5+ Male; 9+ Female
Leads: 7
Setting: Sister Margaret's house/church in Harlem
Length: Three acts

Synopsis

Baldwin's *The Amen Corner* is the story of a tumultuous week in the life of a pastor of a small African American congregation. Sister Margaret is the popular leader of her church; her congregants sing her praises in act 1 as she preaches to them during the Sunday service. She announces to the congregation her intention to go to Philadelphia to help a fellow pastor who has fallen sick. Despite the praise the parishioners offer, however, we quickly learn that Margaret's support is not universal. Another elder of the church, Sister Moore, takes the side of Sister Boxer, who wants her husband to take a job driving a liquor truck. Sister Margaret won't hear of it, arguing that you can't lead people to heaven while trafficking in sin; she sharply rebukes both the Boxers and Sister Moore for challenging her on the issue. The seeds of dissent are sown.

Meanwhile, Margaret's son, David, a promising young musician, is struggling with his own problems. His father—Margaret's husband, Luke, a jazz musician she left years ago—has returned to town to play, and David is drawn to him and the world he represents. Other musicians who have heard him playing for Sister Margaret's church have offered him a place in their touring jazz group. Torn by his love of music and his mother's unyielding disapproval, David loses his faith in his mother's religion and begins to pull away. This break is brought to the forefront when Luke appears at the church, deathly ill but seeking some sort of reconciliation with his wife and son.

The dissenting faction within the church, acting behind Margaret's back even as they claim to be doing the Lord's work, organize a meeting to remove Margaret. Backbiting and hypocrisy abound as they use Luke's sin-ridden life and David's desire to follow his own path as evidence of Margaret's unsuitability. Margaret, helplessly watching David leave her and overwhelmed with mixed emotions at Luke's return, questions her own fitness and is unable to turn the hearts of the congregation back to her. The play ends with Sister Moore celebrating the return of the pulpit, in her words, to the Lord's hands, the congregation singing, and Margaret at the bedside of her dead husband, her son gone, and her world destroyed by her own pride combined with the hypocrisy of the churchgoers.

Key Content Areas

No one escapes blame in *The Amen Corner*. The message Baldwin seems to be conveying is the difficulty of surviving in a complex world and the danger of turning to an extreme, good or ill, to solve problems that are in shades of gray. Sister Margaret believes she loses her husband and her first baby by being too permissive; she overcompensates and loses her son and her church by demanding unyielding righteousness.

Potential Connections/Ideas

The Amen Corner's depiction of a fall from grace involving stubbornness and pride brings to mind both the classic Greek play *Oedipus Rex* and the events surrounding the resignation of President Richard Nixon. Melville's *Moby Dick* also tells the story of a character (Ahab) so afflicted by a personal loss that he destroys himself and all those around him. Margaret's struggle to maintain control of her son as a way of dealing with her own past is similar to the effort Troy Maxson makes in August Wilson's *Fences*.

Although Margaret's internal conflict is central to the text, connections may also be made with the external conflict she faces. The double-dealing and backstabbing in the congregation are similar to the hypocrisy of the townspeople of Guellen in Dürrenmatt's *The Visit*, who find "rational reasons" to murder one of their longtime friends in exchange for promised millions. Hypocrisy is also exposed in Joseph Heller's famous novel *Catch-22*, and the viciousness people are capable of is similarly cloaked in piety and moral outrage in Thackeray's *Vanity Fair* and Hawthorne's *The Scarlet Letter*.

Red Flags

Some references to sexual activity, but nothing crude. (The play is, after all, set in a church.) The mixture of religion and hypocrisy portrayed in the play, however, may pose problems in particularly religious school districts.

Suggested Grade

Suitable for all high school students, who will empathize with David's struggle to find his own identity and recognize the same pettiness that spreads rumors and tarnishes reputations for fun in the maliciousness of Sister Moore and the Boxers.

Critical Readings

Kinnamon, Keneth. Introduction. *James Baldwin: A Collection of Critical Essays*. Englewood Cliffs, NJ: Prentice Hall, 1974. A good general background on James Baldwin and the themes in his works.

Olson, Barbara K. "'Come-to-Jesus Stuff' in James Baldwin's *Go Tell It on the Mountain* and *The Amen Corner*." *African-American Review* 31 (1997): 295–98. An interesting comparison and evaluation of Baldwin's feelings regarding the church in the two texts.

Sylvander, Carolyn. *James Baldwin*. New York: Ungar, 1980. 89–97. Chapter 6 ("The Communion Which Is the Theatre") contains a brief discussion of the purpose behind *The Amen Corner* and Baldwin's means of achieving it.

The Beggar's Opera
John Gay

1728

Characters: 14 Male; 14 Female
Leads: 7
Setting: London, 1728
Length: Three acts

Synopsis

Peachum, the organizer of a gang of thieves and criminals, has decided that Captain Macheath is too much of a risk to let live. He decides to "peach" him for the next session, where Macheath will surely be hanged as a thief. His daughter Polly, however, is in love with Macheath and has been secretly married to him, which makes Peachum fear Macheath all the more, for Macheath can now gain his fortune if Peachum is hanged. He thus resolves to turn to his friend Lockit to have Macheath taken immediately, and Lockit happily obliges by using Suky Tawdry and Jenny Diver, two women of questionable morality, to trap him. Macheath is brought to jail, where we learn he has already impregnated Lockit's daughter Lucy and promised to marry her. This produces further trouble for Macheath when Polly comes to visit her jailed husband and the two ladies meet. Polly and Lucy are once again heartbroken, however, when Macheath is recaptured and sentenced to hang. All is set right, though, as the author steps in and, in accord with the taste of the town, writes a happy ending.

Key Content Areas

As a satire, *The Beggar's Opera* is a masterwork, poking fun at both the theatrical styles popular at the time and the political figures and machinations of the day. It is also the first known example of the "ballad opera," which used popular songs of the day as music, with new lyrics written to fit the scenes.

Potential Connections/Ideas

First and foremost, *The Beggar's Opera* is a satire. It can easily be paired, both musically and in text form, with short examples from other period works (Handel's Italian operas were particularly popular) to demonstrate the parodic and satiric in Gay's work. The work could (and should) also be set in its historical context, linked with the satires and critiques of Pope and Swift, such as *The Rape of the Lock* and *Gulliver's Travels*.

The political side of the play should not be ignored, either; teachers might arrange a lecture from a European history teacher on the somewhat shady politics of Walpole's government.

Part of the beauty of *The Beggar's Opera* is Gay's ability to turn distinctly lower-class characters into suitable material for a farcical opera. Contrasting these characters with those of Hugo in *Les Miserables,* for example, might also prove enlightening. What leads to the changing perceptions of writers? Is Gay actually suggesting that the lower classes are heroic in some ways, or is he simply using them to poke fun at the aristocracy?

One of the best techniques for teaching revision is to use "modernized" or "adapted" plays in conjunction with the originals. Bertolt Brecht's version of John Gay's play, *The Threepenny Opera,* largely retains the original plot and characters, adapting them to twentieth-century Germany. The content in Brecht's version, however, is more adult in character, and teachers may find it beyond acceptable limits for their school.

Red Flags

Frequent "sluts," "whores," and lewd suggestions occurring around the women of the play might offend some female students.

Suggested Grade

Not complicated, but keeping the politics in mind while reading the work may prove too hard for younger students. Tenth-graders and higher should have few difficulties, however.

Film Versions

The Beggar's Opera. Dir. Peter Brook. 1953. (NR)

The Beggar's Opera. Dir. Jonathan Miller. BBC-TV, 1983. (NR)

Critical Readings

Bronson, Bertrand Harris. "From *The Beggar's Opera.*" In *Twentieth Century Interpretations of the Beggar's Opera.* Ed. Yvonne Noble. Englewood Cliffs, NJ: Prentice Hall, 1975. 80–87. Looks at the social satire of *The Beggar's Opera* and the variety of targets it strikes.

Gilman, Todd. "*The Beggar's Opera* and British Opera." *University of Toronto Quarterly* 66 (1997): 539–61. An academic (but still readable) discussion of Gay as a pioneer trying to establish a "British" form of opera through intertwining serious composition using traditional British ballads with lampoons of the Italianate operatic form.

Noble, Yvonne. "Introduction." *Twentieth Century Interpretations of the Beggar's Opera*. Ed. Yvonne Noble. Englewood Cliffs, NJ: Prentice Hall, 1975. An engaging and informative discussion of the political and social conditions leading to the publication of *The Beggar's Opera*.

A Bold Stroke for a Wife

1718

Susanna Centlivre

Characters: 8 Male; 3 Female
Leads: 3
Setting: London, 1700s
Length: Five acts

Synopsis

Centlivre's play opens with a pair of men, Colonel Fainwell and his friend Freeman, sitting in a tavern. The colonel reveals to Freeman that he has fallen in love with a woman he has met at Bath, a Miss Ann Lovely. Although the lady was amiable, he says, she could not bestow either her hand or her fortune of thirty thousand pounds unless all four of her guardians—Modelove, an old beau; Periwinkle, a silly virtuoso; Tradelove, a stocktrader; and Prim, a Quaker—agree on her suitor. The four, however, are all completely different, and each vows never to let Miss Lovely marry anyone but one he recommends. Freeman and the colonel, however, hatch a plot to deceive all of the guardians and win the hand of Miss Lovely. In turns, the colonel impersonates a man of fashion, a Dutch merchant, a collector of scientific curiosities, and a traveling Quaker, convincing each guardian to give consent by acting as everything but the soldier he is. He and Ann are happily united, and all are eventually reconciled.

Key Content Areas

Like the bulk of eighteenth-century Restoration comedy, at the core of *A Bold Stroke for a Wife* is the ridicule of folly. From underneath, however, occasionally peeks the frustration and resentment of women who are forced to depend on the whims of fools for their future.

Potential Connections/Ideas

This play is not what we might consider a "deep" drama. It is a romantic comedy, and, as such, it offers little in terms of themes to explore. I would therefore suggest using this play instead to expand students' historical understanding of the development of drama. You might make it part of a sequence of dramas, moving from a Shakespearean comedy such as *Twelfth Night* or *As You Like It* to a Restoration comedy such as this one, then on to a late-eighteenth-century play such as Sheridan's *School for Scandal* or Goldsmith's *She Stoops to Conquer,* and finally to a modern-era comedy, such as Oscar Wilde's

The Importance of Being Earnest or even a Gilbert and Sullivan operetta, and examine the differences in the romantic comedy from century to century. Have romantic comedies changed significantly? Another option might be to connect this play with other works from the same period by female writers (e.g., Aphra Behn, Mary Pix, Delarivier Manley) and examine them to learn more about the way women perceived their own situation during the eighteenth century. Such a class might tie in well with a history class covering the same period in English history.

Red Flags

None. Most Restoration comedy offers little that can offend.

Suggested Grade

Suitable for any grade, provided the teacher is willing to put in the effort to make now-obscure words and phrases understandable to the students.

Critical Readings

Frushell, Richard. "Marriage and Marrying in Susanna Centlivre's Plays." *Papers on Language and Literature* 22 (1986): 16–38. As implied by the title, a discussion of Centlivre's characterizations of the problems of forced marriage, improper marriage, or attempts to thwart love from a woman's point of view. Argues that Centlivre's work marks a transition from the Restoration to the "modern" period of drama.

The Cherry Orchard

1904

Anton Chekhov

Characters: 7+ Male; 5+ Female
Leads: 5
Setting: Madame Ranevskaya's estate in the Russian countryside
Length: Full play

Synopsis

The Cherry Orchard opens with the return of Lyubov Andreyevna to her home in the Russian countryside. Things have gone very badly for Lyubov and her daughters, Anya and Varya. Their money is all but gone; Lyubov's husband has stolen her remaining fortune and run off, forcing the sale of the estate to be scheduled. Lyubov's family are no help; her aunt isn't willing to bail the family out, and her brother, Gayev, is too foolish and easily confused to be of help. Only Lopakhin, a businessman long fond of Lyubov and interested in marrying Varya, has the potential to help. He grew up on the estate as a peasant; now he is the only one with the money or clarity of thought to preserve the estate.

Unfortunately, none of the other characters are interested in Lopakhin's plan—cutting down the cherry orchard that surrounds the estate, leveling the house, and leasing the land for summer cottages. Lyubov and her retinue, Charlotta and Yasha, don't seem to realize that their money is gone and spend as if everything is just as it has always been. Varya desperately tries to get them to economize, but it is clear from the start that there is no hope.

Similar frustration is present in the love affairs in the household. Anya and Trofimov, a self-proclaimed professional student, are in love but cannot admit it. Dunyasha, the maid, is on the verge of accepting the proposal of the hapless Yepikhodov, but is swept off her feet by Yasha, only to be discarded later. Varya and Lopakhin are fond of each other and have been declared a match by everyone, but Lopakhin never seems to get around to proposing to her; business always gets in the way, distracting him.

The action comes to a head when the auction is forced upon the family by their own refusal to act on Lopakhin's plan. Instead of dealing with the impending loss, Lyubov hosts a party for the town elite, but only the stationmaster and the postal clerk attend. While the festivities are underway, Lyubov anxiously awaits word from the auction, hoping that the sale will bring some sort of hope for them. Gayev returns with Lopakhin, who reports that he has purchased the estate himself. The news crushes Lyubov, who knows her beloved cherry orchard is destined for destruction at his hands.

The next day, the family is packed and ready to depart. As the various sets of lovers take their leave, the distance between Lyubov and Gayev's world and Lopakhin's is made abundantly clear. He celebrates, waving a bottle of champagne about and marveling at his rise, while the others say good-bye to their home and their past happiness. As they leave for the train to Paris, all they have is hope for a change of fortune, but even that is bleak at best.

Key Content Areas

Chekhov's play depicts the slow descent of the upper class in Russia as the business class takes control of their world. The inability of the elite to cope with the changing world produces the tragedy of the play—the destruction of the cherry orchard. The loss of the estate is symbolic of the loss of a portion of the culture, one that cannot be imitated by the new landowners, who think in terms of profit, not history. In that sense, it is a realist piece, providing no happy ending or clear resolution of the characters' fates.

Potential Connections/Ideas

The Cherry Orchard can be connected to a number of texts, particularly others that attempt to present a case study or snapshot of life, such as Upton Sinclair's *The Jungle,* Stephen Crane's *The Red Badge of Courage,* and Anna Deavere Smith's *Fires in the Mirror.* Students might compare the subject matter of these texts with that of Chekhov's play and discuss the common ground between them.

The Cherry Orchard can also be paired with plays about broken dreams that stem from the tragic flaws of the main characters. The classic example of this form is Arthur Miller's *Death of a Salesman,* but Lillian Hellman's *Toys in the Attic,* Ibsen's *The Master Builder,* and Tennessee Williams's *The Glass Menagerie* all feature similarly dysfunctional characters whose shortsightedness hastens their own destruction. Other Chekhov plays that follow the same pattern include *Uncle Vanya* and *The Three Sisters.*

Red Flags

None.

Suggested Grade

Tenth grade and up. The text is easy enough to follow, and the plot clear, but Chekhov's claim that his play is a comedy may puzzle students who haven't had an introduction to drama and the definitions of comedy and tragedy.

Critical Readings

Hahn, Beverly. *Chekhov: A Study of the Major Stories and Plays.* New York: Cambridge UP, 1977. A good general introduction to the themes of Chekhov, containing useful biographical information as well as criticism on *The Cherry Orchard.*

The Crucible

1968

Arthur Miller

Characters: 11 Male; 10 Female
Leads: 6
Setting: A number of houses, a courtroom, and a jail in Salem, Massachusetts, 1692
Length: Five acts

Synopsis

The Crucible opens with Abigail and her uncle, Reverend Parris, standing at the bedside of Parris's daughter, Betty. Parris stumbled on Abigail and Betty out in the forest with some of their friends, dancing—a serious offense to the Puritans. Betty fell into a fit when he appeared and hasn't moved or talked since. Parris is concerned that she may be under the influence of something sinister, and rumors of witchcraft have begun to spread through the village. Parris is more concerned about his reputation than about his daughter and tries to put a lid on the rumors, but when other members of the congregation arrive and insist their daughters are under the Devil's power, Parris tries to bully Abigail into a confession. When Parris goes downstairs to calm the crowd, Abigail slaps Betty and demands that she stop the charade. We quickly learn that Abigail was indeed practicing witchcraft, calling down a curse on Elizabeth Proctor, the wife of the man with whom she has had an affair. She cautions all the girls involved to keep quiet, or she'll kill them herself.

With the arrival of Reverend John Hale, an authority on witchcraft, Abigail finds herself pinned into a corner. She confesses, but places the blame on Tituba, the Jamaican kitchen-woman of Parris's household, who she says is in league with the Devil. With her confession, Abigail is welcomed back to the side of righteousness, and Tituba now faces hanging—unless she confesses to having seen someone else with the Devil. Under this pressure, the helpless woman reluctantly gives in and confesses, but the searchers are not content until she names others who were in league with the Devil. At last, Tituba names one of the older women in the community. Betty and Abigail, seeing an opportunity to escape all punishment, quickly begin crying out the names of other women in the community, and the arrests begin.

John Proctor, a local farmer with a stubborn streak, dismisses the entire story as nonsense, but things soon grow personal for him when he rejects Abigail's approaches. Already ridden with guilt for his early adulterous affair with the girl, he tells Abigail that it will never happen again and that he is well aware of the truth behind her current story. This angers Abigail, who blames Elizabeth, his wife, for her rejection and for her poor reputation around the town. She plots to accuse Elizabeth of witchcraft by having Mary Warren, one of the dancers and the Proctors' housemaid, leave a small poppet with a needle in its stomach in the household. When Abigail is suddenly wracked with stomach pains during the trial sessions, she accuses Mrs. Proctor of the assault, and a warrant is issued.

Proctor, livid that the accusations of a girl are being accepted against the word of long-standing members of the community with unblemished reputations, challenges the accusations. He confesses to Reverend Hale that he had an affair with Abigail, and tells him that Abigail admitted to lying about the events in the forest to avoid punishment. As supporting evidence, he forces Mary Warren to confess that the girls have been acting as if people in court were "attacking" them by spirits. The clergyman, scandalized by the thought he has been deceived and that innocent people are at risk, asks John and Mary to go to court to testify. When they arrive, they give their testimony, but Abigail and the other girls pretend that Mary Warren is controlling them, and when the judge in charge of the trial threatens to imprison Mary Warren if she doesn't release them, Mary Warren changes sides again, accusing John Proctor of controlling her spirit and forcing her to attack the girls. Proctor, stunned, is arrested by the court, which is unwilling to admit that it might have been deceived for fear that it may be held accountable for those who have died under its judgment.

Proctor is imprisoned, and he is told that his only hope of surviving is to confess that he is in league with the Devil. He is offered the chance for pardon if he will admit to the crime but told he will certainly hang otherwise. Reverend Parris, who has come to see that the charges are all false but is no longer able to stop the court, pleads with him to sign the confession, as do others. Abigail and the other girls have fled the town, as public sentiment has turned against the court following the execution of many of the townsfolk, and even the court is beginning to doubt its position. Judge Hathorne tells Proctor that all he needs to do to rejoin his wife—now revealed to be pregnant—is to confess. Broken, Proctor agrees to do so, but he balks at signing a confession to be posted publicly. In a final tearful scene with his wife, he asks for her forgiveness, and she tells him that he has had it for years but never accepted it. When the court insists that the confession cannot stand if not published, Proctor tears it up. Finally in possession of his pride again, he refuses to sacrifice it to survive and goes to his death with confidence as the curtain falls.

Key Content Areas

The Crucible is a play that operates on two levels—literally and as a parallel for the McCarthy hearings and the "Red scare" of the 1950s. As a representation of the trials, the play points out the fundamental unfairness of the hearings, which demanded that those who wanted to avoid being blacklisted as communists provide the names of communists for the committee to investigate. Given such rules, Miller shows, the innocent will surely fall victim to those seeking to keep themselves safe. The validity of a court that operates under such rules is as transparently absent as that of the Salem courts that executed women on the strength of accusations alone. Taken at face value, Miller provides a drama which explores the power of fear and guilt on the human psyche and the rarity of the mental strength needed to make a hero.

Potential Connections/Ideas

The Crucible can be taught in several ways. One approach is to incorporate it into a study of Puritan literature, alongside works such as Cotton Mather's *Wonders of the Invisible World* (an account of the Salem witch trials) or the sermons of Jonathan Edwards, particularly "Sinners in the Hands of an Angry God." Miller's play is realistic enough that students will be able to use the text to discuss Puritan values and laws. This discussion would ideally be accompanied (possibly through team teaching with the school's history department) by historical background on the difficulties facing communities during this period. Such an examination will help to explain the power that religious leaders seem to have in the community and the harsh laws of the time. Miller also took liberties with history in creating this play, however, and any good discussion of the historical context of *The Crucible* has to explore where Miller made changes and why he felt the need to do so.

A second approach would be to take the play solely as a parable for the McCarthy era. Doing so allows the teacher to integrate it into the unit covering that period in American literature or, alternatively, to use it as part of a unit on censorship in the arts and the period of the infamous blacklists. In either case, teachers might turn to historical material on the period, including film of the McCarthy hearings themselves (widely available on videotape), to give students an idea of the atmosphere Miller was trying to capture. An ensuing discussion on the various means of censorship, from direct bans on material to indirect forms of censorship, such as attacks on the character of the author, limiting the distribution of the material to make it virtually inaccessible, or enacting laws that directly affect the material in question, would be a valuable opportunity to bring students to consider their own complicity in censorship. Do they do things that silence other voices, knowingly or unknowingly?

Finally, *The Crucible* is an excellent play to use to teach the basic form of drama. Its five acts follow the pattern of rising and falling action perfectly, with reversals or climaxes in each act that help raise tension as the play progresses. Miller captures the essence of his subject matter; the reader cannot help feeling terror at what has been unleashed as Act 1 ends with Betty and Abigail calling out the names of every woman who has ever crossed them, or when John Proctor is betrayed by Mary Warren and the court is too concerned with its own reputation to admit its error. John Proctor, too, is an excellent example of a protagonist, developing from a bitter, stubborn man who closes his heart rather than examine it into a powerful, heroic figure who dies at peace with his wife and himself.

Red Flags

The scene in which Abigail reminds John of their sexual liaison is suggestive, though not excessively so. Teachers should review it and use their discretion.

Suggested Grade

The only obstacle this drama presents is the length of the piece; it may be too long for younger readers to maintain focus. Still, it is no longer than one of Shakespeare's plays, and we regularly present those to ninth-graders. As a major work effectively covering two periods of American literature, *The Crucible* is usually taught as part of the American literature curriculum in eleventh grade, but it would be effective in any high school class.

Film Versions

The Crucible. Dir. Nicholas Hytner. With Winona Ryder and Daniel Day-Lewis. 1996. 124 minutes. (PG-13)

Critical Readings

Evans, Richard I. *Psychology and Arthur Miller.* New York: E. P. Dutton, 1969. A series of interviews between Evans and Miller, touching on many of Miller's thematic and social foci, including the writer's role in political and social commentary.

Steinberg, M. W. "Arthur Miller and the Idea of Modern Tragedy." *Arthur Miller: A Collection of Critical Essays.* Ed. Robert W. Corrigan. Englewood Cliffs, NJ: Prentice Hall, 1969. A crucial essay exploring Miller's conception of the modern tragic figure—a common man who struggles to preserve his dignity against the forces of the universe.

Warshaw, Robert. "The Liberal Conscience in *The Crucible*." *Arthur Miller: A Collection of Critical Essays.* Ed. Robert W. Corrigan. Englewood Cliffs, NJ: Prentice Hall, 1969. A strong attack on the liberal audiences of Miller's day and on what Warshaw sees as the weaknesses of Miller's play. Argues that Miller manipulates the historical context to suit his needs but ends up undercutting his parallels in search of so-called universality.

Death and the King's Horseman   *1975*

Wole Soyinka

Characters: 9 Male; 4–6 Female
Leads: 3
Setting: A Yoruba city in Nigeria, 1943
Length: Five acts

Synopsis

Elesin, honored among his people as the man designated "King's Horseman," is busy celebrating as the play opens. He has the best of everything in the community—food and clothes are his for the asking, and women gladly accept his requests for their company. His Praise-Singer, with the matron of the tribe, Iyaloja, reminds Elesin that though he is their leader he must not forget the price of that leadership—that he is supposed to "commit death" and join his dead king, and that failure to do so will bring a terrible curse upon his people. Elesin assures them that he will be able to live up to the task (so to speak), and a night of singing and preparation begins.

Elesin clearly intends to follow through with the ritual, but not everyone on the island accepts the Yoruba ritual as appropriate. Simon and Jane Pilkings, the British officer assigned to govern the colony and his wife, learn about the upcoming suicide rite and take steps to intervene. Amusa, a Yoruba now working for the English as a police officer, reveals Elesin's plan, and soldiers arrest the King's Horseman on the verge of his completing the ritual.

The arrest triggers a riot, as the villagers mourn the curse to come. Elesin, stripped of his honor despite his lack of control over the situation, is imprisoned; his son, Olunde, returned from his studies in England to bury his father, refuses to acknowledge his existence. Iyaloja and others in the community come to the prison to heap scorn on Elesin, who protests that he was committed to the ritual until others forced him to abandon it. This argument is dismissed by the community, however, and even his son, who has left behind traditional Yoruba ways to become a physician, is horrified by Elesin's weakness. Abandoned by his people, Elesin mourns his failure, until he learns that his son has committed suicide on his behalf. Devastated and racked with shame at the sight of his son's corpse, he strangles himself.

Key Content Areas

Although Soyinka's foreword to the play specifically warns against assuming that issues of colonialism are at the heart of this play, it is impossible to ignore the interference of the British that seems to be the major cause of the tragic events. The failure of the English to try to understand the Yoruba is crucial to the action and to interpretations.

Potential Connections/Ideas

Death and the King's Horseman won the 1986 Nobel Prize for Literature. When dealing with award-winning books, I find that one way to start interesting discussions is to ask students why they feel the book won an award and if they agree with the assessment. Of course, to make an informed decision, the class may need to talk about what the Nobel Prize is and what it is meant to reward. They may then need to explore the historical and political issues that are involved in the play to judge Soyinka's efforts. An understanding of the issues surrounding colonialism, for example, would be a good goal for a bridge effort between a history classroom and an English classroom.

Students might also wish to discuss the actions of Elesin's son, Olunde. The characters in the play seem to expect Olunde to have abandoned his culture because he traveled to England to study medicine. Instead, the well-educated man reverts to the "primitive" ways, finishing the ritual suicide in place of his father. Does Olunde's choice surprise students? Do they respect the decision? Can we justify such rituals in a modern, "humanist" society?

There is a growing body of colonial and postcolonial literature available for classroom use, works that could be incorporated into a unit on the topic or simply as a supplement to the individual works. *Things Fall Apart*, by Chinua Achebe, is the classic novel in this genre, but you could easily work in texts like Maxine Hong Kingston's *The Woman Warrior* or Brian Friel's *Translations*, each of which explores the challenges of a minority culture faced with impending assimilation or acculturation. You might even contrast Soyinka's tragedy with John Patrick's *The Teahouse of the August Moon*, a play that treats the American occupation of Okinawa as nothing more than a pesky annoyance for the Japanese and that is written by a member of the invading culture, not the native culture.

Red Flags

One reference to excretion, and a few sexual references.

Suggested Grade

The language gets a little flowery at times, but it isn't beyond the ability of an interested class. Once again, the historical background is helpful and may improve the students' experience with the text. Tenth grade and up.

Critical Readings

Maduakor, Obi. *Wole Soyinka: An Introduction to His Writing.* New York: Garland, 1986. Chapter 11, *"Death and the King's Horseman,"* is a view of the text on three levels: his technique, his use of language, and the play as a drama of transition. It is written in moderately academic language but is still understandable to those outside of post-graduate academic research.

Reed, Ishmael. "Soyinka among the Multiculturalists." *Black American Literature Forum* 22 (1988): 705–9. An angry (but well-crafted) condemnation of what Reed saw as the racist intellectual response to Soyinka's play.

Soyinka, Wole. Author's note. *Death and the King's Horseman.* Contains information on the history of the play and the incident it is based on.

Death of a Salesman

1949

Arthur Miller

Characters: 8 Male; 5 Female
Leads: 5
Setting: Loman's house, 1949
Length: Three acts

Synopsis

Willy Loman, the protagonist of *Death of a Salesman,* is a man who is surviving on his dreams alone. The play opens with his return to the house, where we learn that he hasn't been able to work as a traveling salesman for some time. Linda, Willy's wife, urges him to ask for a local, nontraveling position, and Willy reluctantly agrees. He begins to ask about his sons, Biff and Happy, and quickly begins to rant angrily about Biff's lack of a suitable job. He overlooks Happy completely and continues to do so for the remainder of the play.

Biff has been searching for a job, traveling in the West, but hasn't been satisfied with anything he's found. He is a former high school athlete who failed his last class—math—and never made up the credit in summer school. His scholarship offers disappeared, and he is now 34, jobless, and unsure of what is missing in his life. He harbors terrible antagonism toward Willy, which is explained later in the play in a flashback scene where Biff walks in on Willy on the road in Boston, intending to tell him about his failing math grade, and discovers him having an affair.

Willy is unable to accept that his sales career has been fruitless, his sons unsuccessful, and his status as role model destructive. He is slowly going mad, and flashbacks from his memories interweave with the current action to show us where the mistakes were made that bring Willy to the brink of suicide. We see him pumping up his sons with lies and encouraging them to behave destructively. We watch him ignore Happy and celebrate every success Biff has, never calling him on the carpet for failing math or for stealing from the school. We watch Biff's image of his father deflate when he discovers that Willy is cheating on his mother. Finally, we watch Willy's pride keep him from real job offers from friends, even as the company he works for pushes him away. Willy's dreams and pride cannot bear the revelation that Biff finally forces on him—that he and his son are failures.

Willy is broken by this revelation, but at the same time sees the love his son has for him and the pain he is in. In an act that both cheapens and redeems him, the father deliberately kills himself in an auto "accident," leaving his sons with $20,000 in insurance money and a new start. Sadly, as the two stand with their mother at Willy's grave, we see that Biff has grown and has a chance but that Happy, always ignored by his father, has completely absorbed Willy's personality in a bid for attention and seems destined for the same fate.

Key Content Areas

Is Willy Loman a tragic hero? The value of Miller's protagonist and his culpability in his own downfall and that of his sons are the center of this play.

Potential Connections/Ideas

Willy Loman's status as tragic-pathetic figure is often paralleled with Oedipus, the tragic hero of *Oedipus Rex*, whose pride brings about a terrible fall from grace. A more modern example of this type of tragic collapse under the weight of frustration comes from Miller's contemporary, Lillian Hellman, in *Toys in the Attic*.

Jane Smiley's *A Thousand Acres* is the story of an older man who, in trying to create a legacy, destroys his family. His pride forces confrontations among his daughters, and those confrontations result in death and broken lives. Additionally, Miller's creation of a character simultaneously both tragic and pathetic can also be seen in John Knowles' *A Separate Peace*, in which the protagonist, Gene, slowly explains to us that he destroyed his best friend's life out of pure jealousy. We sympathize with his guilt and want to forgive his crime, but at the same time we reject him as admirable because of the flaws he acknowledges. Finally, the speaker in Robert Browning's famous poem "My Last Duchess" delivers a lecture to his companion on the painting of his former wife, telling us of the murder he has committed as if it were the most natural thing in the world; he, like Loman, persuades himself that everything is fine, even as those who listen to him condemn him as a madman.

Red Flags

Some sexual innuendo; Biff and Happy talk about the number of women they've slept with. Willy's lover appears on stage in her underwear.

Suggested Grade

Death of a Salesman is best for seniors. Although it would make a sensible addition to the traditional junior year American literature curriculum, the subject matter—the future and the reality of its expectations of you—will be more immediate for seniors, who are approaching a major transition. Seniors will also be more set in their definition of "hero," and Willy Loman may prove difficult for them to easily classify and dismiss.

Film Versions

Death of a Salesman. Dir. Laszlo Benedek. 1951. B&W, 115 minutes.

Death of a Salesman. Dir. Volker Schlondorff. With Dustin Hoffman and John Malkovich. 1985. 130 minutes. (PG)

Critical Readings

Bloom, Harold, ed. *Arthur Miller's* Death of a Salesman. New York: Chelsea House, 1988. A collection of essays on *Death of a Salesman,* running the gamut of interpretive directions. Of particular interest are Bloom's introduction, Esther Merele Jackson's essay on the play as a modern conception of the tragic myth, and Brian Parker on Miller's use of contrasting points of view.

Roudané, Matthew C. "*Death of a Salesman* and the Poetics of Arthur Miller." *The Cambridge Companion to Arthur Miller.* Ed. Christopher Bigsby. New York: Cambridge UP, 1997. 60–85. An overview of the themes of falling, family, and myth in Miller's play and a discussion of how staging can complement these themes.

Steinberg, M. W. "Arthur Miller and the Idea of Modern Tragedy." *Arthur Miller: A Collection of Critical Essays.* Ed. Robert W. Corrigan. Englewood Cliffs, NJ: Prentice Hall, 1969. A crucial essay exploring Miller's conception of the modern tragic figure— a common man who struggles to preserve his dignity against the forces of the universe.

Degas, C'est Moi

1995

David Ives

Characters: 3+ (up to 12) Male; 3+ (up to 12) Female
Leads: 1
Setting: An open stage, with a gray wall at rear, the present day
Length: One act

Synopsis

Degas, C'est Moi is a short comedy that opens with Ed, an undistinguished man of inde-terminate age, sitting on his bed. On the spur of the moment, he decides that for the day, he is going to be Edgar Degas, the great French impressionist painter. At once, he begins to consider his "ordinary" life through the lens of Degas, considerations we are made privy to by way of slides projected on the gray wall behind Ed.

Ed's wife, Doris, and the other people Ed encounters don't seem to notice Ed's transformation. He proclaims his Degas-ness to the world, and it goes utterly unrecognized. His dry cleaner is unmoved; the unemployment clerk doesn't notice the name change until Ed points it out, and the man at the betting window at the track couldn't care less if Ed pays in francs or dollars. Ed dismisses the absence of recognition at first, wondering if the first Degas didn't experience much the same thing.

In search of more information on himself, Ed heads for the library and then to the museum. At a local doughnut shop, for a brief moment, he sees a young woman who looks at him and sees—Degas! Just as quickly, she is gone. Later, as Ed eats dinner with Doris, he begins to feel Degas slipping away from him, the persona fading with the day. At home, Ed sees himself again and realizes that not only is he not Degas, he is nothing at all. His presence, like Degas's, is forgettable, no more and no less for the dif-ference in fame. At that moment, sitting on the bed, he looks at Doris, fresh from the shower, and sees her with the same color and vibrancy as Degas would, but through *his own* eyes, realizing for the first time that that vision comes from within, not from a name.

Key Content Areas

The uplifting message of *Degas, C'est Moi* is that the realization of the beauties of the world and the vision of a great artist don't go hand-in-hand with artistic skill. Rather, the sense of the color, vibrancy, and essential life of everything around us comes from a willingness to see it—no more, no less.

Potential Connections/Ideas

Degas, C'est Moi shares common ground with a number of works. Teachers could begin by connecting the quick changes of set and scenes largely created through the actor's behavior and audience cooperation to the sketchy sets of the Shakespearean stage and to more experimental pieces, such as Anna Deavere Smith's *Fires in the Mirror.* Such pieces offer opportunities to discuss the benefits and drawbacks of small-stage or small-set productions.

The content of Ives's play also offers opportunities for connections. The need for the individual to find internal strength rather than relying on an externally created identity or social approval is crucial to Ralph Ellison's *Invisible Man* and to James Joyce's *A Portrait of the Artist as a Young Man.* Novels like Kate Chopin's *The Awakening*, Virginia Woolf's *Mrs. Dalloway*, Zora Neale Hurston's *Their Eyes Were Watching God*, and Nathaniel Hawthorne's *The Scarlet Letter* all deal with this issue as well, but primarily from a woman's perspective. Arthur Miller's classic work, *Death of a Salesman*, asks a slightly different question—where does personal worth come from? Is it a product of self-respect, or must it come from external affirmation?

Finally, the style of *Degas, C'est Moi* is strongly reminiscent of the works of Neil Simon or Woody Allen, writers who skillfully use self-deprecating comic heroes to convey a larger point. The advantages and disadvantages of comedy and tragedy in presenting a theme or idea could be the source of a short discussion or a unit-length investigation, depending on the goals of the teacher, the interests of the students, or the time constraints on the class.

Red Flags

Profanity occurs in two places. Though played for comic effect and only briefly present, the language used is not mild. I include this play, however, despite the profanity, because of an increasing tolerance in public schools for texts that include such language if it is used in service of an artistic end, and because the language can be easily excised or altered for classroom use in school systems that do not permit its use. While I am not an advocate of censorship, I am also unwilling to discard a play entirely on the grounds that I teach the "true text" or nothing at all. Teachers must use their judgment in deciding where the line between the two is drawn, and whether the lost words significantly alter the meaning or presentation of the text.

Suggested Grade

With the profanity excised, *Degas, C'est Moi* is suitable for all high school students. Its positive message may help teens who are struggling with a need to define themselves in terms of social recognition. Ives's fast-paced, comic style will appeal to older students as well.

A Doll's House

1879

Henrik Ibsen

Characters: 6 Male; 5 Female
Leads: 5
Setting: The Helmers' apartment
Length: Three acts

Synopsis

Nora is the flighty wife of Torvald Helmer, a lawyer just raised to the position of bank manager. Nora is delighted at this turn of good fortune, because for years she, her husband, and their three children have had to struggle to survive on a very small salary. This struggle was complicated by a debt Nora had incurred from another bank employee, Nils Krogstad. Krogstad lent Nora $1,200 to take Torvald to the south for a year to recover from overwork, a debt she concealed, claiming instead that she got the money from her father, who had died at the time. Now Torvald is the bank manager, and her debt is almost repaid; Nora finally feels freedom is approaching.

Trouble is visible in the Helmer household at once. Torvald treats Nora like a pet, calling her his "little songbird," mocking her inability to keep track of money (money that has been going to repay the debt, unbeknownst to him), and even trying to regulate her diet. He sees himself as taking care of his beautiful wife, and Nora seems delighted to let him do so. Behind the scenes, though, we see that Nora clings to her secret debt not only as something Torvald would be horrified by but also as a source of power over her husband. She was the one who came up with the money to save him, not her father. She made it possible for him to live. This secret knowledge gives her tremendous pleasure, and she proudly shares it with Kristina Linde, a widowed friend who comes to ask for a job from Torvald.

Torvald agrees to take on Mrs. Linde, planning to use her to replace Krogstad. Torvald despises Krogstad because Krogstad forged a signature years ago, and Torvald's rigid morality knows no forgiveness. When he learns of Torvald's plans, however, Krogstad comes to Nora and asks her to intercede. When she refuses, he produces her debt bond and points out that she forged her father's signature on it after his death. Unless she prevents the loss of his job, he will reveal her crime to the world. Nora agrees to try to help, but Torvald will not hear of taking his wife's advice. Not only does he dislike Krogstad but also he fears people will laugh at him for being under his wife's thumb. Nora tells Krogstad of her efforts, but he posts a blackmail letter to her husband anyway.

Mrs. Linde pries the story out of Nora and goes to appeal to Krogstad herself. Years ago, she had thrown him over for a husband with money, so she could support her brothers and her mother. Now a widow, she asks him to put aside his claim on

Nora, marry her, and let her support him with her job at the bank. To do so, she says, would give her reason to live again. Krogstad, still in love, agrees and sends the bond back to Nora with a note of apology.

In the dramatic final scene of the play, Nora tries to flee the house to commit suicide before Torvald reads the first letter, so that he cannot try to sacrifice himself for her. He stops her, however, and angrily berates her, calling her a liar and a criminal. He will do as Krogstad asks, and she will continue to live there for appearances, but she will no longer raise his children or be regarded as his wife. Nora watches him coldly as he reads the second note from Krogstad and joyously rips up the bond she owes him. The threat averted, Torvald tells Nora that all is forgiven and that he will just have to be even more careful to take care of her now. Nora, however, has had enough. Torvald's reaction to the first note from Krogstad—to worry about how he will be hurt, not about her situation—disappoints her, and his willingness to pretend nothing has happened after the threat to him is averted angers her. Pointing out that Torvald has, like her father, treated her like a doll to be admired and cared for, Nora tells him that she no longer loves him and that she needs to leave him to become a real person. Despite his protests that he can change and that she owes a duty to her children and husband, she leaves him as the curtain falls.

Key Content Areas

A Doll's House demonstrates the confining role of the wife and how crushing to the spirit it can be. Ibsen's strong argument against the treatment of women as simple objects that men must care for caused an uproar in many communities; in Germany, the play was even given a new ending in which Nora stays out of loyalty to her children. The play is one of the earliest examples of a feminist statement in a drama, although Ibsen's comments at a banquet in 1898 that his work was never about issues, but instead about people, has often been interpreted as a denial of intentional support of feminism.

Potential Connections/Ideas

Marriage slowly crushes Nora Helmer's spirit in *A Doll's House* until she is forced to contemplate suicide and flee the household to regain her individuality. This is a theme repeated in a number of literary works, one of the most popular recent examples being Janie's realization in Zora Neale Hurston's *Their Eyes Were Watching God* that a woman doesn't have to have a husband to be complete, no matter what the community thinks. The same theme is illustrated with different results by Edna Pontellier in Kate Chopin's *The Awakening;* unlike Nora, her crime is adultery, brought on by boredom and a need to assert independence, but, like Nora, she refuses to continue living in a loveless marriage as a slave to duty.

Teachers might wish to use *A Doll's House* as part of a study of the development of the female voice in literature. There is no doubt that Nora, however flighty early on in the play, is one of the first independent heroines in literature, and teachers might present her along with other early examples of strong women, such as the Wife of Bath in the *Canterbury Tales,* Portia in *The Merchant of Venice,* and Dorothea Brooke in *Middlemarch.* Early female writers who could also be drawn on as source material for a unit on the development of a female voice include Marie de France, composer of the early romantic stories, the *Lais of Marie de France;* Hannah More and the other Blue Stockings, a group of women devoted to learning and scholarly discussion in the late eighteenth and early nineteenth centuries; and Mary Wollstonecraft, author of *A Vindication of the Rights of Woman.*

Red Flags

None.

Suggested Grade

A Doll's House is appropriate for all high school students and is ideal for starting discussions of representation of minorities in literature early in a student's academic career. The earlier students begin to consider such issues, the better equipped they will be for a truly multicultural classroom.

Film Versions

A Doll's House. Dir. David Thacker. TV version, 1991. 136 min.

A Doll's House. Dir. Patrick Garland. 1973. 105 min. (NR)

A Doll's House. Dir. Joseph Losey. With Jane Fonda. 1973. 106 min. (NR)

Critical Readings

Templeton, Joan. "The *Doll's House* Backlash: Criticism, Feminism, and Ibsen." *PMLA* 104 (1989): 28–40. Argues that Ibsen was advocating feminism with Nora in *A Doll's House* despite what she sees as a misreading of his 1898 comments on the issue by many critics.

Fences   *1986*

August Wilson

Characters: 5 Male; 2 Female
Leads: 4
Setting: 1957, a house in a back alley of a big-city neighborhood
Length: Two acts

Synopsis

Fences opens with Troy Maxson, a man who never quite achieved his dreams, and his best friend, Jim Bono, coming home from work on a Friday night. We learn that Troy used to play baseball but never quite made it to the major leagues because of an "injury." The true reason that Troy was locked out, of course, was his race; black ballplayers, however good, could not play in the major leagues. Now Troy has a job as a trash collector, and even in that position, he finds his avenues of advancement blocked by racism, as only the white employees are assigned to drive the trucks, and the black collectors are relegated to riding on the back and doing the heavy lifting. Though his union holds out hope for his advancement, Troy is wary of trusting any authority.

He seems happy, though, with a good relationship with his wife, Rose. Bono, however, is concerned that word has gotten around that Troy has been spending too much time talking to another woman. He warns him not to lose what he already has, but Troy doesn't take his warning seriously. Meanwhile, Cory, Troy's son, is offered a football scholarship and a chance to attend college, but Troy tells him that he needs to learn a skill like auto repair instead so that he can get a good job. His past frustrations keep him from seeing that with the college scholarship Cory has a shot at offers with far more advancement potential than Troy's path, and Rose is unable to persuade him.

When Cory defies him and continues to play football, Troy cancels the appointment with the recruiter, leading to a confrontation between Troy and Cory, which Troy wins, though barely. The wedge this drives into the family relationship is worsened when Troy announces that he has fathered a baby by the other woman and that he wants to care for it as a father should. Cory leaves to join the military, and Troy and Rose are left to raise Troy's child, whose mother has died in labor. In the final scene, the grown child meets the estranged Cory at Troy's funeral and realizes that his father wasn't perfect, but he was a decent man who tried to do right.

Key Content Areas

The family and family relations, of course, are at the center of the play. Discussion might center on Troy. Is he a hero? Or is he a character in the Willy Loman, *Death of a*

Salesman mold, one for whom we feel some sympathy but who we feel is too weak or too culpable for his situation to treat as a hero?

Potential Connections/Ideas

Fences might be paired nicely with *Death of a Salesman,* leading up to the comparisons between Troy and Willy that I suggested. There are, however, several other options. There is a strong resonance between the father–son relationship of Troy and Cory and that of James Tyrone and his son James Jr. in Eugene O'Neill's autobiographical play, *Long Day's Journey into Night.* Some novels focusing on families in conflict that *Fences* may bridge to include Jane Austen's *Mansfield Park,* in which a daughter struggles to escape her family's social ineptitude; Robertson Davies's comedy *Leaven of Malice,* about the son and the daughter of feuding families who find themselves engaged to be married, courtesy of a prank announcement in the local paper; or the Kiswana Browne segment of Gloria Naylor's novel *The Women of Brewster Place,* in which a daughter tries to explain to her mother her need to spend time living in a poorer black neighborhood instead of her old middle-class home.

It is also worth noting that August Wilson was offered the opportunity to write a film screenplay for *Fences,* and that Eddie Murphy was prepared to play the part of Cory in a major studio production. Wilson, however, insisted that the film be made only with a black director, and this led to extensive debate over the notion of race as a qualification for acting or directing certain material. Wilson was taken to task by many for saying that he felt that African American actors should perform only in Afro-centric plays, instead of taking parts in the traditional productions that already dominate the stage.

Red Flags

Fences contains frequent uses of the word *nigger* spoken among African American characters. This may be offensive to some students, particularly if the reader for the part is white. If you choose to use this play, a short discussion regarding Wilson's use of the word in this context may be useful.

Suggested Grade

With the above caveat, grades eight and up.

Critical Readings

Fishman, Joan. "Developing His Song." *August Wilson: A Casebook.* Ed. Marilyn Elkins. New York: Garland, 1994. 161–81. An interesting discussion of the editing process for *Fences* and the choices and themes revealed through Wilson's drafting choices.

Pereira, Kim. *August Wilson and the African-American Odyssey.* Urbana: University of Illinois P, 1995. An examination of *Fences* in fairly accessible language, particularly the motivations that drive Troy Maxson's behavior to his son and wife.

Fires in the Mirror   *1993*

Anna Deavere Smith

Characters: 20 Male; 8 Female
Leads: None
Setting: Various offices, streets, restaurants; 1991
Length: Twenty-nine monologues

Synopsis

Fires in the Mirror is a series of connected monologues, developed out of interviews Anna Deavere Smith conducted following the incidents in Crown Heights, New York City, in August 1991. The circumstances were tragic: A car in the motorcade of the head of the Lubavicher sect of Judaism, Rebbe Menachem Schneerson, is involved in an accident that forces the car off the road. It strikes and kills a seven-year-old Guyanese American boy, Gavin Cato. Three hours later, an angry mob of black youths surround a Lubavicher visiting from Australia, Yankel Rosenbaum, and he is stabbed repeatedly. He dies later that night at the hospital. A youth is charged with the stabbing but is subsequently found not guilty of the attack. The grand jury refuses to bring charges against the driver of the car, who leaves the country for Israel before he can be questioned. The ensuing protests on both sides result in hundreds of arrests.

Smith's monologues, taken from interviews with witnesses and community members, fill in the perspectives and motives of both the sides involved with unflinching honesty. Each attempts to preserve the language of the speaker, as well as the content of the interview. Among those who "speak" as part of the production are Caramel Cato, Gavin's father; Reverend Al Sharpton, the well-known activist; Rabbi Joseph Spielman, spokesman for the Crown Heights Lubavitch community; Norman Rosenbaum, Yankel Rosenbaum's brother; and numerous members of the community. Smith makes her work even more powerful by relying primarily on figures who wouldn't normally be heard in the debate—an anonymous black youth, an anonymous Lubavich woman, a community program leader. The depth produced by the wide swath of interviews lends credibility to Smith's neutral position as observer-reporter.

Smith has since produced *Twilight: Los Angeles, 1992,* a similar one-woman show examining the Los Angeles riots in 1992 following the acquittal of four Los Angeles police officers on all but one charge resulting from the videotaped beating of Rodney King.

Key Content Areas

Race and race relations are central to this incident, particularly the growing rift between the formerly closely allied African Americans and Jews. The general plight, however, of both groups as they try to exist as minority cultures in America is also considered. If a lesson is to be drawn from these monologues, it is that there may be two "true" sides to the story.

Potential Connections/Ideas

Fires in the Mirror is a powerful play that is likely to provoke animated discussions of who's right and who's wrong. Such judgments are too simple for the complexities of the Crown Heights incident, but a teacher can easily turn the snap judgments into an advanced discussion of the gray areas we all encounter in our lives and how we deal with them.

For those interested in using *Fires* as a bridge, I would suggest tying the play to other texts that deal with the conflict of strong emotional issues and justice. Nonfiction options include articles on the Clarence Thomas–Anita Hill debate or the more recent move to end affirmative action programs. Fiction that might be appropriate includes *Native Son* by Richard Wright, Wole Soyinka's *Death and the King's Horseman,* and Brian Friel's play *Translations.* Younger readers might appreciate this play more if they first read and discuss the problematic conflicts in books such as S. E. Hinton's *The Outsiders* and John Knowles's *A Separate Peace.*

You might also desire to explore monologues further; I recommend seeking out one of the many actors' books available, such as *The Actor's Scenebook.* Other artists who have produced one-man or one-woman shows include Eric Bogosian and Spalding Gray, although their works should be carefully screened by the teacher to identify sections appropriate for teenagers.

Red Flags

Aside from the obscenities in this production (some fairly vulgar), teachers should be concerned about the potential emotional impact of this play in the classroom. Ensure that in discussion, care is taken for all students' feelings, particularly in classrooms with Jewish and African American students.

Suggested Grade

I'd be careful about bringing this play into a classroom. It should be suitable and beneficial, however, for any class that has shown the maturity needed to deal with the complex issues involved without making snap judgments. The value of *Fires in the Mirror* is indisputable, but the content requires care in presentation.

Film Versions

Fires in the Mirror. Dir. George C. Wolfe. 1993. Produced for the PBS *American Playhouse* series. (NR)

Critical Readings

Lewis, Barbara. "The Circle of Confusion: A Conversation with Anna Deavere Smith." *The Kenyon Review* 15 (1993): 54–64. Interview that probes Smith's technique and intent, as well as her views on the black artist in general. The questions in the interview are primarily oriented toward African American issues.

Reinelt, Janelle. "Performing Race: Anna Deavere Smith's *Fires in the Mirror.*" *Modern Drama* 39 (1996): 609–17. An analysis of pose, posture, and production values in PBS's *American Playhouse* production of Smith's play. Focuses on how Smith uses voice, cadence, and posture to create an engaging style that helps to disarm those who would critique her fairness.

The Glass Menagerie

Tennessee Williams

1945

Characters: 2 Male; 2 Female
Leads: 4
Setting: The Wingfield apartment, located upstairs in a St. Louis tenement
Length: Seven scenes

Synopsis

The Glass Menagerie is a play made up of Tom Wingfield's memories, specifically those of the events that led up to Tom's eventual break with his family. The scene opens with Tom standing in front of a gauze wall, through which we dimly see the Wingfield apartment. Tom tells us about the characters in the play, and then the wall slowly begins to rise as the scene begins.

Over dinner, Tom's mother, Amanda, begins to reminisce about her youth and the pleasure of receiving visits from a variety of potential suitors. Tom's demeanor tells us that this is a frequent topic, but Amanda soon turns the discussion to Laura, Tom's sister, and her preparations to receive callers that evening. Laura tells her mother that she is not going to receive a caller; no one has ever come calling, and she doesn't expect that to change. Amanda, though, refuses to listen or to accept that her daughter's painful shyness and her leg brace significantly reduce her chances for marriage.

The extent of Laura's shyness is made clear when we learn that for the last six weeks she has been pretending to go to a school to learn typing but in fact has been sitting in the park instead. On her first visit to the school, she became so nervous that she vomited; she hasn't been able to face returning. Amanda, frustrated, points out that, if the two of them are to survive, Laura needs a career—or a husband. Laura admits there was a boy in the past who interested her, a fellow high school student named Jim. Amanda, seizing on the news, decides that finding a match for Laura is the only course to follow. She begins to save and to raise money by selling magazine subscriptions, and she asks Tom to help as well.

Tom is tremendously frustrated, a man nearing the end of his rope. He writes poetry, and he wants to experience the world, but his income from his factory job is necessary for Laura and Amanda's survival. His only escape from his mother's dream world and his sister's constant nervousness is the movie theater, a vice he regularly indulges for hours on end. When his mother confronts him about his late nights and insists that she doesn't believe he's just at the movies, Tom snaps and storms out of the house, accidentally breaking some of Laura's prized collection of glass figurines.

The next day, Tom apologizes for his outburst, and agrees to help find his sister a caller. He brings home a friend of his from the factory—James O'Connor. James, as it happens, is Laura's Jim from high school, and Laura is terrified when she finds out. She almost fails to make it to dinner but, through her mother's contrivance, is eventually forced to sit alone with Jim and talk to him. He remembers her from high school and slowly draws her out of her shell. Laura shows him the menagerie, talks with him about her life, and in the process begins to grow more and more confident. Jim sees the change and tells her that she ought to have more confidence in herself. He tells her she is quite pretty and, in an impulsive moment, kisses her to make his point.

Laura is stunned at her good fortune and is clearly completely in love. Jim sees this at once, however, and immediately tells Laura that he would be delighted to go out with her under other circumstances but that he has a steady girlfriend he's in love with. He quickly makes his departure, aware of the pain he's caused. Amanda, learning what has happened, calls Tom in and demands to know how he could have been so foolish as to invite a man with a steady girlfriend to call on his sister. Tom is stunned by the news; he was unaware that Jim was in a serious relationship. Amanda doesn't believe him, however, and begins to scold him furiously. When he puts on his coat to go to the movies, hoping to escape his mother's caustic comments, she redoubles her attack, calling him insensitive and selfish. Unwilling to take her abuse any longer, Tom smashes his glass to the floor and storms out, leaving the two forever. As he reflects on what he left behind and the memories that he couldn't, however much he wanted to, the lights fade out.

Key Content Areas

Tennessee Williams strikes a remarkable balance in *The Glass Menagerie*. Although his characters evoke sympathy from the audience—Tom is stuck in a dead-end job that is crushing his soul because of his responsibility to his family, Laura's disability and shyness are a combination that effectively paralyzes her socially, and Amanda's pride is still recovering from her husband's abandonment of the family—Williams also forces us to acknowledge their own role in their suffering. Amanda is so caught up in her past that she fails to recognize the pain Tom suffers or the impossibility of what she demands from Laura. Laura, for her part, demonstrates with Jim that she can transcend her fears but cannot find the strength or confidence to do so on her own, and thus she continues to place the burden of her support on her brother. Tom doesn't recognize that his drudgery allows the status quo to continue and that he is effectively hiding his own insecurities about his writing by allowing the movies to substitute for his life. In sum, *The Glass Menagerie* is about the difficult choices we have to make and the occasional unpleasantness of life we must accept to truly live.

Potential Connections/Ideas

Williams is often described as a Southern Gothic writer, and his work nicely complements that of William Faulkner. Both authors deal in a dark vision of frustrated lives and a decaying world. For teachers looking to compose a complete unit that includes Williams, however, a more concrete focus would be the tension between duty and individual desire in the human spirit. Chopin's *The Awakening* explores this theme, as does Hansberry's *A Raisin in the Sun.* Noël Coward's one-act play *Fumed Oak* follows a comic variation of this theme, and Samuel Beckett reduces this tension to absurdity in *Waiting for Godot* by creating two characters who are absolutely unable to act on individual desire and allow their lives to be defined by their dutiful waiting for the never-arriving Godot.

An alternate approach to *The Glass Menagerie* is to connect it with other works that detail the frustrations of the working-class world. These include the plays of Clifford Odets, particularly *Awake and Sing!* and *Waiting for Lefty;* the Charles Dickens novel *Hard Times;* Lillian Hellman's drama *Toys in the Attic;* and *A Portrait of the Artist as a Young Man* by James Joyce. Students could compile a list of their own methods of escapism or ways of coping with the unchangeable frustrations in their lives and compare their responses to the ways in which the protagonists in each work choose to deal with the obstacles in their paths. Is Tom right to leave his family? At what point does satisfying yourself become more important than your duty to relatives?

Finally, the semi-autobiographical nature of *The Glass Menagerie* may offer an opportunity to work the play into self-discovery projects and units. Students might investigate how Tom's life parallels Williams's own and develop autobiographical pieces of their own to express ideas they want to share. Teachers who take this approach should also be prepared to discuss the interaction between fiction and nonfiction in an autobiographical text: How much artistic liberty does the writer have?

Red Flags

Two highly objectionable words used to describe African Americans appear in the opening scene. Teachers should point out that such language, although completely unacceptable today, was part of Southern culture at the time, although it reveals a great deal about Amanda's privileged Tennessee upbringing.

Suggested Grade

Juniors and seniors. Younger students will likely find the play slow and without bite, whereas older students can discuss Tom's desire to escape in terms of their own search for personal identity and how it conflicts with the demands placed on them by parents and other authority figures.

Film Versions

The Glass Menagerie. Dir. Irving Rapper. With Kirk Douglas. 1950. B&W. (NR)

The Glass Menagerie. Dir. Anthony Harvey. With Katherine Hepburn, Michael Moriarty, and Sam Waterston. 1973. Made for TV. (NR)

The Glass Menagerie. Dir. Paul Newman. 1987. 134 min. (PG)

Critical Readings

Bloom, Harold, ed. *Tennessee Williams's* The Glass Managerie. New York: Chelsea House, 1988. Another in the Modern Critical Interpretations series, this collection contains eleven essays on various aspects of *The Glass Menagerie* and its author. Among the most useful are Roger B. Stein's essay on the division between the violent and the nonviolent in Williams's work and essays by Lester A. Beaurline and Geoffrey Borny, both writing on the revision of the short story "Portrait of a Girl in Glass" into the two forms of the play (a "reading" version and an "acting" version) that are in print today.

Siebold, Thomas, ed. *Readings on* The Glass Menagerie. San Diego: Greenhaven Press, 1998. A collection of fourteen essays on *The Glass Menagerie,* dealing with a variety of issues and themes, including illusion and reality, loneliness, social commentary, and freedom.

Goodnight Desdemona (Good Morning Juliet)

1988

Ann-Marie MacDonald

Characters: 2 (9) Male; 3 (6) Female (*Numbers in parenthesis indicate parts if multiple roles are not assigned*)
Leads: 5 (15)
Setting: An office, present day; Cyprus (*Othello*); Verona (*Romeo and Juliet*)
Length: Three acts

Synopsis

Goodnight Desdemona opens in the office of Constance Ledbelly, a longtime graduate student with little hope of ever completing her thesis, mostly because she spends her time penning works for her "advisor" (and the man she loves in vain), Claude Knight. After learning that Knight is not going to marry her or promote her, she finds herself alone, depressed, and perusing a strange manuscript. As she reads, she finds herself drawn into the action—literally—of Shakespeare's *Othello*, through a magical "warp" in her wastebasket. Arriving in Cyprus, Constance quickly learns that Desdemona isn't quite the hapless heroine found in our versions of the story.

Indeed, in this version of the play, Desdemona is a fierce warrior, on her way to fight invaders when Constance appears. Spotting Iago about to deceive Othello, Constance intervenes, revealing Iago's treachery and earning Othello and Desdemona's friendship. Desdemona in particular takes a liking to Constance, believing her a virgin oracle from a land of Amazons. Iago, however, isn't finished causing trouble. Determined to make Constance pay for his disrupted plans, he convinces Desdemona that Constance actually has designs on her husband. Madly jealous, Desdemona hurries off to kill Constance, but before she can, Constance is whisked off to Verona by another strange "warp."

There, in the midst of *Romeo and Juliet,* Constance finds herself pursued by *both* love-smitten title characters! Tired of each other, the two teens are both searching for new love and find the strange "young man" (Constance arrives in tights) entrancing. Mischief ensues as Constance tries to flee both oversexed characters, only to find Tybalt stalking the man he believes seeks to dishonor his cousin by sleeping with her husband. Juliet is on the verge of committing suicide for her love (though she has no need to, as Constance repeatedly points out), and Desdemona, who pursued Constance through the "warp" to Verona, by turns tries to kill and woo her former friend. Finally, Constance finds her own strength as she considers the flaws of each of her favorite heroines, deciding to reject both of them. Chastened, the two agree to try to learn some restraint, and Constance, realizing that she, unlike the characters, has it within her to be author of her own destiny, returns to her office shaken but wiser.

Key Content Areas

MacDonald addresses two major content areas in this comedy, gender and historical perspective. In terms of gender, MacDonald offers us a woman used by men and the academic system who finds strong role models in two of Shakespeare's female characters, who are completely subject to the men in their lives. There is a clear critique of the male hierarchy, paralleled by a background attack on the assumptions scholars make about the "truth" of certain documents, without examining who wrote them and why.

Potential Connections/Ideas

MacDonald's play is probably best used as a follow-up to either *Othello* or *Romeo and Juliet,* more likely the former because it is traditionally taught in higher grades. You could plan a lesson on Desdemona or Juliet, exploring their characters and why Shakespeare didn't really develop either one. A discussion of MacDonald's incorporation of Shakespeare's work might make a nice bridge to genre discussions of pastiche, parody, or perhaps even satire. From that discussion, a teacher could turn to novels that parody or to rewritings of original stories, such as John Gardner's *Grendel* or Jane Smiley's *A Thousand Acres.* A more comedic option might be *Rosencrantz and Guildenstern Are Dead,* which would open up discussions of marginal characters to include both genders. Of course, the option always exists to set up a creative writing assignment for students, asking them to "rewrite" a traditional play into something a bit different.

Red Flags

Goodnight Desdemona is not scrupulously clean, but it isn't David Mamet, either. Expect the occasional expletive ("Bullshit" becomes Desdemona's battlecry, for example) and several references to sex and sexual orientation, particularly in the *Romeo and Juliet* act—though most are veiled in pseudo-Elizabethan verse. Even so, if you aren't prepared to deal with the notion of lesbianism in your class, skip this play.

Suggested Grade

The play itself is not too hard to follow, but the sexual content and the background issues might may more sense to those in grades ten and up.

Critical Readings

Porter, Laurin R. "Shakespeare's 'Sisters': Desdemona, Juliet, and Constance Ledbelly in *Goodnight Desdemona (Good Morning Juliet)." Modern Drama* 38 (Fall 1995): 362–77. An extensive analysis of the play as a groundbreaking feminist revision of Shakespeare's female characters.

The Hairy Ape

1921

Eugene O'Neill

Characters: 10+ Male; 2+ Female
Leads: 1
Setting: A steam-driven cruise ship and New York City, 1921
Length: Eight scenes

Synopsis

In *The Hairy Ape,* Eugene O'Neill presents a tale of a man whose pride is shattered when he is made to see himself for the first time through the eyes of those wealthier and more powerful. Yank is a stoker for a transatlantic cruise ship. He and his fellow crewmen shovel coal into the furnace to drive the ship, a job Yank convinces himself to take great pride in. Though the workers live in miserable conditions, covered in and breathing coal dust, singed by furnace blasts, and unable to even stand upright in the low-slung compartments they live and work in, Yank seems to glory in his place. He dismisses the rich as idle; they live off the work he does. He is the only real man on board—the source of energy for all of society. With fervor, he argues that he is the steel out of which civilization is built and that the engines move only because he makes them move. Without him, everything would grind to a halt.

Yank's faith in his own value, however, falters badly when Mildred, daughter of the cruise line owner, takes a visit down to the furnace room to see "how the other half lives." When she enters, she finds Yank swearing at the engineers who are demanding more speed from the stokers, and the raw, brutish Yank scares her terribly. She shrinks away from him, hiding her face in horror. Yank, who hadn't realized that she was there, turns to see her horrified at his looks and behavior, and he is dumbfounded. As she is hurried out, however, he realizes that he has been insulted and begins to threaten vengeance. His pride is badly shaken; convinced that she viewed him as nothing more than a "hairy ape" in a menagerie, he begins for the first time to doubt his place as the moving force in the universe. While he continues to rage and bluster, we can see that the violent outbursts are Yank's attempt to win back his self-esteem.

Angrily, the stoker goes into New York's fashionable Fifth Avenue district the next time he is in port. There he attempts to pick a fight with some of the rich men he feels have insulted him, but they roundly ignore him. Yank is soon arrested and thrown into jail—a double indignity, as he realizes the cage that holds him is the same steel he had earlier claimed to be made of, now mockingly keeping him in place like a sideshow animal.

Once out of jail, Yank tries to join the Industrial Workers of the World, hoping to become a part of the violent actions against the wealthy that the newspapers claim the

IWW coordinates. His open admission that he wants to destroy buildings for the IWW makes the Wobblies believe that he is an infiltrator, and they kick him out. Rejected by workers and upper class alike, Yank finds himself at the zoo, talking to the gorilla and considering how he must appear to the rest of the world. Taking the ape for his brother in arms, he breaks the lock on the cage and releases the animal, but it turns on him at once, crushes him, and tosses him into the cage before shuffling off. There, behind the steel bars of a cage at the zoo, Yank dies, sarcastically calling people to come and view the great hairy ape.

Key Content Areas

O'Neill's play shows how the pain of a working man's life comes not from the job itself but from a loss of pride and dignity. He contrasts the faked, pallid world of the upper class, with its robotlike citizens who complain about the absence of energy and honesty but who run when confronted with it, to the real energy and fierce pride of a worker who has nothing else to keep him going.

Potential Connections/Ideas

The Hairy Ape can be approached in a number of ways, depending on the requirements of the unit the teacher is composing. As a play about the importance of pride in keeping a person going, it can be paired with a number of works about African American pride, such as Langston Hughes's classic poem "Harlem (A Dream Deferred)," Lorraine Hansberry's play *A Raisin in the Sun*, Anna Deavere Smith's play *Fires in the Mirror*, or Zora Neale Hurston's novel *Their Eyes Were Watching God*. Each carries as a theme the disastrous effects of a loss of self-worth and the extraordinary efforts people will make to preserve that self-worth.

As an exploration of the life of the working class and the social burden produced by social division, *The Hairy Ape* would work well in conjunction with any of Clifford Odets's highly political plays about labor, such as *Waiting for Lefty*. In many ways, Yank resembles the simple but well-meaning Lennie in John Steinbeck's *Of Mice and Men*. Both men are strong and love their work, and both have their worlds suddenly disturbed by the unexpected appearance of a woman not of their class. Each dies as a result of the encounter, never quite understanding why.

On its own, *The Hairy Ape* can be taught as an extended Darwinian metaphor. With his title and with the conclusion, O'Neill seems to be challenging us to identify just how it is that we have progressed from the apes, and whether Yank represents the high or the low end of the progression. What characteristics make someone human? Why does the world act as if Yank doesn't possess them?

The Hairy Ape can also be used to teach the differences between "realist" and "symbolist" theater. Is this a realistic depiction? Is Yank meant to be taken at face value, or does he represent something greater?

Red Flags

Several *damn*s, but no more serious profanity. Of more concern is the use of stereotypical racial epithets among the stoking crew; although most will be unrecognizable to the average student, care should be taken to point out that they are used not to degrade but to show how dehumanized the stokers are. Few have names any longer; they are simply identified by their country of origin. Any worker could be Yank on any given day.

Suggested Grade

Nothing in the play makes it unsuitable for younger students, but the thrust of O'Neill's critique may be lost on ninth- or tenth-grade students. Juniors and seniors, however, should be able to see the various levels on which the play operates, particularly if a connection can be made to their own frustrations with low-level service jobs.

Film Versions

The Hairy Ape. Dir. Alfred Santell, 1944. B&W. 92 min. (NR)

The House of Bernarda Alba 1936

Federico García Lorca

Characters: 0 (2–3 offstage) Male; 17 Female
Leads: 8
Setting: Two rooms and a patio in the house of Bernarda Alba
Length: Full play

Synopsis

Antonio Maria Benavides has passed away, leaving his wife and his five daughters and one of the best estates in the small town where they live. With his death, his iron-fisted widow, Bernarda, declares that the family will go into mourning, shutting themselves in for the next eight years out of respect for the dead. Bernarda has lost all interest in love and marriage, dismissing them as frivolities and the paths to dishonor. No man in the town is worthy of her daughters, so she will keep them all under lock and key to ensure that they do not dishonor themselves with an inappropriate match.

The daughters, of course, resent their mother's stifling rules; none save Adela, the youngest of the five at age twenty, is beautiful, but none save Angustias, the eldest at thirty-nine, has money or property. All are desperate to get out of their mother's home, to break free and find love, and when love comes, they are quick to turn on each other.

Young Pepe El Romano comes to the house seeking wealth by wooing Angustias, to the frustration of Bernarda, who accuses Angustias of being little more than a harlot for trying to find a man the day of her father's funeral. Bernarda quickly comes to terms with the match, and the family prepares for the marriage, but Pepe has other plans. When he visits Angustias, he stays afterward and visits Adela as well. The two begin a secret love affair, planning to live as man and mistress after Pepe and Angustias marry.

Martirio, another of the sisters, falls in love with him as well, watching Pepe and Angustias and then Pepe and Adela from her window. She confronts Adela, warning her that she will reveal the affair to their mother if Adela doesn't leave Pepe alone. Adela, however, is desperate to leave and has the confidence of youth on her side; she dares Martirio to try to stop her and forces her to admit that she loves Pepe herself. Martirio denies that this is the reason she wants to stop Adela, however; it is for the sake of honor, not envy, that she intervenes.

As the wedding draws near, Adela slips out of the house to meet Pepe on a night he is supposed to be out of town instead of visiting Angustias. Martirio, still watching her, catches Adela and blocks the door; when Adela won't return to the house, Martirio screams for help. When the straw from the barn stuck on Adela's skirts gives away her relationship with Pepe, Angustias lunges for her at once. Bernarda, grabbing her shotgun, tries to shoot Pepe but misses, succeeding only in chasing him away. Adela flees into the house, knowing the affair is over, and blocks the door. When the others finally force their way in, they find the young woman has hanged herself. Bernarda, in tears, orders her cut down and laid out in a white dress, declaring that her daughter died a virgin and ordering the others to keep silent about the entire incident—but silence has already fallen on the house.

Key Content Areas

In Lorca's play, the focus is on the stifling atmosphere that Bernarda creates for her daughters. Bernarda, we learn, has been a victim as a wife; she wasn't loved by her husband, who turned to the maid for sexual gratification, and she instead immersed herself in the Church and in the family's need to maintain its social position. Her morality is intractable, unfettered by the need to love or be loved. When she forces this on her daughters, however, Lorca demonstrates that, however well intentioned her actions are, Bernarda has done to them what her husband did to her—forced them to live without love or hope of release. The young women are thus forced to rebel in order to break their mother's lock on their lives, and they do so, with disastrous results.

Potential Connections/Ideas

The House of Bernarda Alba can be used as part of the world literature curriculum, expressing one of the dominant themes of Spanish literature—passion and social order at a crossroads. Within the context of a world literature classroom, however, teachers will probably want to connect Lorca's play to similar works to create or supplement a unit. Based on the theme of the play, *The House of Bernarda Alba* would be a good fit with Dickens's *Great Expectations,* Yukio Mishima's short Noh play, *The Damask Drum,* Emily Brontë's *Wuthering Heights,* or even Shakespeare's *Romeo and Juliet.*

Another approach is to focus instead on the family relationship in the play. Bernarda's domination of the family to the point of tyranny forces the younger characters into action, with tragic results. Arthur Miller's *Death of a Salesman* covers much the same ground, with Willy Loman's refusal to see the true nature of himself and his sons leading to their unhappiness and failure, and eventually his own death. *The Glass Menagerie,* one of Tennessee William's greatest plays, also follows the slow destruction of a family as Amanda, the mother, tries to force her daughter, Laura, to relive her own youth and her son, Tom, to give up his future to make it possible. Eventually, Laura's fragile self-esteem is shattered by her mother's machinations, and Tom is driven from the house altogether in a last-ditch effort to save himself. This theme is at the center of Shakespeare's *King Lear* as well, and this play makes an excellent linchpin for a unit on intergenerational struggle.

Red Flags

A woman is beaten to death for having a baby out of wedlock and then killing it; a young woman hangs herself.

Suggested Grade

As a play about frustrated lovers, Lorca's piece seems well suited for ninth graders as a companion to *Romeo and Juliet,* but Bernarda's motives may not be understandable to younger readers. By tenth grade, however, students should be able not only to understand the play but also to identify with the passions and frustrations of competing for romantic interests.

Film Versions

The House of Bernarda Alba. 1976. UK TV production.

The House of Bernarda Alba. Dir. Stuart Burge. 1991.

Critical Readings

Klein, Dennis A. Blood Wedding, Yerma, *and* The House of Bernada Alba: *García Lorca's Tragic Trilogy.* Boston: Twayne, 1991. A complete overview of *The House of Bernarda Alba,* including historical background and discussion of structure, characters, and themes. Includes a bibliography.

Iago

1979

C. Bernard Jackson

Characters: 1–4 Male; 1–4 Female
Leads: 2
Setting: A theater, present day
Length: Full play

Synopsis

Iago opens with the lead male, the Author, addressing the audience as he would a college English class. We are informed that we have come to this place to get the real story of Othello, Shakespeare's famous character, in the interest of scholarly accuracy. Iago's wife, Emilia, enters and agrees to tell the story, but only if the audience and Author participate. She, four Entertainers of ambiguous sex, and the Author reenact the story of Othello as it actually occurred, and we learn that Shakespeare changed a great deal of the story. Iago is no Venetian; he is a Moor like Othello. Cassio, not Iago, is the villain of the story, drinking on watch, calling Iago an ape, and eventually betraying Othello when he falls from favor. He accuses the general of treachery and rouses the Venetians to kill the Moorish troops in their sleep. As the tragedy unfolds, Iago stabs the Author, currently playing Cassio, and as he bleeds, the Author realizes that this is no play for Emilia. Badly wounded, he tries to leave the cast, explaining that he was there only to judge for himself and write his own version of the story. Infuriated, Emilia and the Entertainers force him to continue, this time as Desdemona. As Othello strangles him/her, the Author again tries to break free, but he is once again recast as Cassio, and then stabbed by the invading Turks. As he dies on stage, this time as Othello committing suicide, Emilia finishes her story, reminding us all that Iago was the hero, not the villain "that Englishman" painted him. Having returned her husband's reputation to him, she allows the play to end.

Key Content Areas

Iago is both a response to Shakespeare's *Othello* and a social statement. It challenges both the specific text that portrays the African general as a hotheaded, easily duped man and the general notion that an author has the right to recount a story from his or her perspective instead of that of the people involved. Indeed, the play questions whether such a retelling is even possible.

Potential Connections/Ideas

Clearly, this text is best taught in tandem with *Othello,* but it could be taught to students who have watched a video of the story or have read a good summary of the action as well, though far less effectively; such students will miss the clever manipulation of Shakespeare's own language in a ploy that causes the play to bring its own validity into question: How can Jackson's critique of an author's rewriting of events be invalid if Jackson does it himself? *Iago* could also be taught as part of a unit on "responses" to existing texts, such as "The Nymph's Reply to the Shepherd" by Sir Walter Raleigh, *Shamela* by Henry Fielding, or *Rosencrantz and Guildenstern Are Dead* by Tom Stoppard. Finally, it could be used to introduce a discussion on the ways authors represent people in their texts. How do we create characters, and how do we avoid stereotyping in doing so? Why, for example, do so many people find *The Adventures of Huckleberry Finn* offensively racist, while others defend it as an antislavery statement?

Red Flags

Repetitions of Shakespeare's sexual references from *Othello* and an indirect reference to Iago's genitalia in Emilia's final speech.

Suggested Grade

Best for eleventh and twelfth grades, when the students have probably encountered this sort of critical literature already and have a basis to discuss the "true" story concept. They may also be better prepared to take seriously the discussion of racial stereotyping that may follow.

The Importance of Being Earnest   *1895*

Oscar Wilde

Characters: 5 Male; 4 Female
Leads: 4
Setting: London; 1895
Length: Three acts

Synopsis

Jack Worthing visits his friend Algernon Montcrieff and tells him of his intent to marry Algernon's cousin Gwendolyn. After explaining to Algy why he has invented a brother named Earnest to impersonate while in the country, he seeks out Gwendolyn's mother, Lady Bracknell, to request her permission. She denies it, however, as Jack can produce only the handbag in which he was left for adoption as a lineage. Algy has meanwhile fallen in love with Jack's ward, Cicely, after visiting her in the character of Jack's invented brother Earnest. Jack, angered by Algy's deceit, reveals to Cicely that Algy is not Earnest, and Algy reveals to Gwendolyn that Jack is not named Earnest either. The two women, refusing to marry men named Algernon and Jack, retire but are reconciled to the men when they both agree to be rechristened Earnest. Lady Bracknell's objections are removed when Jack is discovered to be the lost son (christened Earnest) of her sister (Algernon's mother), left accidentally on a rail platform by Gwendolyn's governess. All are happily engaged to be married as the play ends.

Key Content Areas

The Importance of Being Earnest is one of the great satiric plays of all time. It is an excellent example of what the eighteenth and nineteenth centuries termed "wit." It also contains a great deal of social commentary on the late-nineteenth-century upper class and its behavior.

Potential Connections/Ideas

The Importance of Being Earnest can be used in a number of ways in an English class. As a model of social satire, it can be used as part of a unit on dramatic forms and styles. As social satire, it might be grouped with other works that comment on the manners and behavior of the upper-class English, works that could include Thackeray's *Vanity Fair,* Addison's *Sir Roger De Coverly Papers,* the anonymously written *The Female Tatler,* and Samuel Johnson's *Rambler* essays. Wilde himself was the subject of several burlesques, none so popular as Gilbert and Sullivan's *Patience,* in which he was portrayed as an "aesthetic sham." Studying Wilde's poetry and his famous essay *The Decay of Lying* in conjunction with this parody could lead to interesting discussions regarding Gilbert's assessment. In addition, teachers looking to increase awareness in the classroom regarding alternate lifestyles might point out that Wilde was imprisoned for committing homosexual acts as well as for debt, and discuss his critics in that light as well. (There is an excellent trial scene in the recent movie *Wilde,* starring Stephen Fry, which could prove useful as a starting point for this discussion.)

Red Flags

Nothing to speak of. A very elegant, perfectly proper insult to all that was very elegant and perfectly proper.

Suggested Grade

Grades ten and up, or mature readers in younger grades. Wilde's wordplay and foolishness have significance, but younger students may miss it while trying to follow the witty banter.

Film Versions

The Importance of Being Earnest. Dir. Anthony Asquith. 1952. 95 min. (NR)

The Importance of Being Earnest. Dir. Michael Attenborough and Michael Lindsay-Hogg. 1981. 114 min.

The Importance of Being Earnest. Dir. Kurt Baker. 1991.

Critical Readings

Ellman, Richard, ed. *Oscar Wilde: A Collection of Critical Essays.* Englewood Cliffs, NJ: Prentice Hall, 1969. Contains several biographical pieces on Wilde and his arrest, plus several useful essays on *The Importance of Being Earnest.* Eric Bentley's short excerpt, "The Importance of Being Earnest," is of special note.

Holland, Vyvyan. *Oscar Wilde and His World.* New York: Charles Scribner's Sons, 1960. A thorough account of Wilde's life, most notable because Holland was Wilde's second son and can thus provide family anecdotes otherwise unpublished.

The Jew of Malta

1633[*]

Christopher Marlowe

Characters: 15+ Male; 4+ Female
Leads: 1
Setting: The island of Malta
Length: Five acts

Synopsis

Barabas, the Jew of Malta, is a student of the Machiavellian arts. His life is dedicated to making as much money as possible and to the care of his daughter, Abigail. When the play opens, Barabas, having just received word of huge successes from his last trade missions, is celebrating. A request comes from the Governor that he and all other Jews come to court; when they appear, they learn that Malta is being threatened by the Turks and that the tribute the Turks demand is to be paid by them alone. The Governor orders that half of all the property belonging to a Jew be taken, and for those who refuse, the choice is conversion or confiscation of all their goods. Barabas protests this treatment, but when threatened with confiscation, he agrees to give up half his wealth. The Governor refuses, claiming that one protest is defiance enough, and he confiscates the entirety of Barabas's fortune, even converting his house to a nunnery. Suddenly homeless and penniless, Barabas vows revenge on those who reduced him to this state.

His daughter, Abigail, helps him to this vengeance in two ways. First, she pretends to convert to gain entry to the new convent and recover some hidden gold for her father. Afterwards, she becomes the unwitting tool for Barabas to gain revenge on the Governor. He promises his daughter to Lodowick, the Governor's son, and to the man she loves, Mathias, as well. Using a slave he purchases as the delivery boy, he sends a forged challenge from one lover to the other. The two meet and kill each other in a duel, much to Barabas's delight. Abigail, however, is distraught by her father's actions and the loss of her love, and she returns to the convent and converts.

Barabas is horrified by this turn of events and, using his servant, sneaks a pot of poisoned porridge into the convent, killing all the nuns. As Abigail is on her deathbed, she confesses her part in her father's crime to a friar, who then goes with a friend from another order to confront Barabas. Thinking himself undone, Barabas agrees to convert and offers his money to the order that he will join. The two friars come to blows over the offer, and Barabas sees another opportunity to escape. He asks each to return that night, and when the first comes, he strangles him. He then places the friar outside his door, where the other friar confronts him. Angered at the dead man's silence, the

---

*Published posthumously; first performed c. 1592.

second friar strikes him with his staff, and Barabas and his servant quickly accuse him of the murder of the man. The second friar is hung, and Barabas seems to have escaped again.

Once again, however, Barabas faces doom when his servant deserts him and tries to blackmail him. Before Barabas can escape, he is taken prisoner; although he manages to poison his accusers, he has to fake his own death to escape. Betraying the city to the Turks for his vengeance, he is made governor when they capture Malta and then plots to betray the Turks to the Maltese forces in exchange for one hundred thousand pounds. The ex-Governor agrees but then betrays Barabas, dumping him into the cauldron meant for the Turks and using Barabas's trap to regain control of the island.

Key Content Areas

The message of the play is not so much anti-Semitic as that those who live by treachery die by treachery. Although Barabas is clearly capable of great evil, one cannot forget that he does nothing until the Governor arbitrarily strips him of his wealth and even his home. Then again, Barabas doesn't know when to let things be, and as a result, he is destroyed by his own plotting.

Potential Connections/Ideas

The Jew of Malta is best taught side by side with Shakespeare's *The Merchant of Venice*. The two plays are clearly drawn from the same basic source, but they are different in tone and in their extremity of violence. *Merchant* has no murders and only one major plot involving Shylock, the Jewish antagonist. *The Jew of Malta,* however, is extremely bloody, with no fewer than five deaths on stage, including poisoning, stabbing, strangling, and boiling in oil. Students may also consider the portrayal of the protagonists in each play to determine if the accusations of anti-Semitism leveled against Shakespeare are warranted.

Outside this obvious point of comparison, placing the two plays side by side also provides an excellent opportunity to examine the differences in style between two of the greatest dramatists of the Renaissance. Students can examine the styles of the authors and discuss the importance of those differences. To what audience is Marlowe appealing with his plots? To what audience is Shakespeare appealing? What is the goal of each play—the message each wants to communicate—and how does each playwright pass that message along? Or are they simply trying to entertain?

Of course, there are other options for integrating *The Jew of Malta* into the curriculum. On its own, it is a well-crafted play that can be used as an effective example of tragedy. Teachers might also bring this play in as part of a unit on representations of minority cultures by members of the majority, along with such texts as John Patrick's *The Teahouse of the August Moon* and George Eliot's *Daniel Deronda,* or contrasted with statements of the minority culture, such as Jamaica Kincaid's *A Small Place.* This is a weaker approach, however, than pairing *Malta* and *Merchant;* the two plays taken together offer a rare opportunity to examine great authors in parallel contexts and are worth the reading time needed to look at both texts.

Red Flags

This play has undeniably anti-Semitic elements to it; care should be taken to underscore that this was a sentiment of the period and that both Marlowe and Shakespeare make a point of giving their protagonists some provocation for their actions.

Suggested Grade

With this caveat observed, this play is suitable for all high school students. It is probably best used in a senior English class, when students are practicing placing authors side by side for literary analysis.

Critical Readings

Bevington, David M. "The Jew of Malta." *Marlowe: A Collection of Critical Essays.* Ed. Clifford Leech. Englewood Cliffs, NJ: Prentice Hall, 1964. 144–58. An overview of the logic of the play, focusing on the use of character pairings and on the plot and character devices used to create a world full of villains.

Deats, Sara Munson, and Lisa S. Starks. "'So neatly plotted, and so well perform'd': Villain as Playwright in Marlowe's *The Jew of Malta.*" *Theater Journal* 44 (Oct. 1992): 375–89. Argues that Barabas is Marlowe's voice in an argument over the ethics of the theater at a time when the legitimacy of the form was under assault on both artistic and religious grounds.

Goldberg, Dena. "Sacrifice in Marlowe's *The Jew of Malta.*" *Studies in English Literature 1500–1900* 32 (Spring 1992): 233–45. Discusses the theme of sacrifice and Barabas as sacrificial victim for Malta in Marlowe's play, with reference to the mythos of Judaism and classical biblical allusions.

Humphreys, Arthur. "*The Jew of Malta* and *The Merchant of Venice:* Two Readings of Life." *Huntington Library Quarterly* 50.3 (Summer 1997): 279–93. Explores the parallels and the differences (arguing that the latter far outweigh the former) in the two plays and seeks to explain the natures of the key characters: Barabas as the radiating source of action; Antonio as the passive center on which the action converges.

Macbett

1972

Eugene Ionesco

Characters: 8+ Male; 4+ Female
Leads: 4
Setting: A field, a castle, and a forest, all World War I period or later
Length: Full play

Synopsis

Macbett opens in a field with the meeting of two dukes, Glamiss and Candor. The two denounce the tyrannical rule of Duncan and agree to attempt to overthrow him. Their revolution, however, is defeated after a bloody battle with Duncan's two generals, Macbett and Banco—who incidentally look almost alike enough to be twins. Duncan, accompanied by his wife, Lady Duncan, appears to announce that both Candor and Glamiss should be executed and that Banco and Macbett will receive their titles and lands (less half the property for taxes, of course). Glamiss escapes, only to be drowned in a flood; the cowardly but greedy Duncan uses this as a pretext to bilk Banco out of his promised title and lands, as he didn't perform Glamiss's execution as ordered.

Macbett and Banco each meet two witches in the forest who promise each one power and glory. Macbett is promised the throne and Banco's title; Banco is promised to be father to a line of kings. Both characters denounce the prophecies, but later, after Banco loses the promised title and Macbett gains it, the two agree to overthrow Duncan, each secretly coveting the remainder of their promised gains. Lady Duncan, who is revealed to be one of the two witches, spurs Macbett on by seducing him and promising to marry him after Duncan's death. The three successfully murder Duncan, but before the celebration has even ended, Lady Duncan and the second witch have vanished. Macbett overhears Banco talking about how his children will be kings, and he kills Banco, declaring him a traitor. The ghosts of Banco and Duncan appear before Macbett at the wedding feast that night, informing him that he will soon die. Sure enough, Macol, Duncan's eldest son, returns from taking his degree at Carthage to lead an army against Macbett. He kills the usurper, but just as everyone begins to celebrate, he informs the people present that he will be far worse a ruler than Macbett ever was, quoting extensively from Shakespeare's *Macbeth,* Act 4, Scene 3. The curtain closes as he disappears into a cloud of mist.

Key Content Areas

Ionesco has written a creative and cutting satire of *Macbeth,* exploring many of the same themes. Gullibility, ambition, and the cowardice of military leaders are all explored in

Macbett, but the two most important areas Ionesco seems to explore are the historical patterns of autocratic rule and the ease with which people of the best intentions are perverted. Human frailty and cruelty is put on display for the audience.

Potential Connections/Ideas

The most obvious and the most useful way to teach *Macbett* is as a follow-up to the reading of Shakespeare's *Macbeth*, the play it mimics and parodies. Taught side by side, the two plays show two different views of human nature, with Ionesco taking a much bleaker position despite producing a comedy rather than a tragedy. This could be used as a jumping point for discussing the range of works that can be labeled comic or tragic and the elements in each. Teachers could also use *Macbett* as an example of "taking ownership" of a play through interpretation and thus as a means to encourage students to rewrite parts of *Macbeth* themselves for exploration and interpretation.

   Alternatively, *Macbett* could be taught as part of a unit on twentieth-century literature; it would work well in combination with the caustic sarcasm of Kurt Vonnegut or Don DeLillo. As part of a discussion of absurdism, *Macbett* could be paired with other explorations of apparently pointless cruelty, such as Knowles's *A Separate Peace*. It could be coupled with Tom Stoppard's *Rosencrantz and Guildenstern Are Dead*, Gloria Naylor's *Mama Day*, or Jane Smiley's *A Thousand Acres* as a unit on modern retellings of Shakespeare. Finally, *Macbett* would work well with Swift's *Gulliver's Travels* and Sinclair Lewis's *Elmer Gantry* as examples of political and social satire.

Red Flags

Macbett contains three obscenities, all of the variety that appear in the *Canterbury Tales*. It is a remarkably clean play for a modern production, with only one or two moments of sexual innuendo. There are several on-stage beheadings and murders, but they are comical in effect rather than particularly bloody.

Suggested Grade

This play would be acceptable for grades eight and up, but I would reserve it for tenth- to twelfth-graders, who may be better equipped to understand the parody and dark satire Ionesco uses.

Manfred

1817

George Gordon, Lord Byron

Characters: 5+ Male; 1+ Female
Leads: 1
Setting: The mountains of Switzerland, both inside and outside Manfred's castle
Length: Three acts

Synopsis

Manfred is a dramatic poem in which Byron presents a character tortured by his past but frustrated in his quest for death by the immense magical powers he controls and by his unwillingness to submit to the control of any external force. Manfred is alone in the world; though his castle has attendants, he is friendless and without love or pity. Early on, he bemoans this fate, first seeking out the spirits of the earth and the heavens in search of a means of banishing his memories, and later seeking assurance that his own demise is imminent. Manfred desperately wants to escape the curse that lingers over him, which we learn midway through the play is the death of his beloved, Astarte. The precise relationship between Manfred and Astarte is unclear; whatever bond they shared, however, led to Astarte's eventual suicide. Manfred blames himself for her death and has since had to bear the burden of guilt that now drives him to seek his own end.

Unfortunately, the stubborn refusal to submit to another power limits Manfred, denying him respite even as it defines him as an individual. He purchases his independence at a heavy price, unable to repent and be granted absolution because he will not bow to the divine, and unable to banish his conscience entirely and live dissolutely as he will not purchase his powers and pleasures from the Devil. Death, Manfred hopes, will bring long-awaited peace.

In hopes of abating his guilt, Manfred travels to the hall of the most powerful of the spirits, Arimanes, and demands that the spirit lord raise Astarte's ghost to speak to him. Impressed by the pride and power of the daring mortal, Arimanes agrees, and the ghost appears. Manfred begs her to speak to him and grant him forgiveness for her death, but all the ghost will say is that death will come to him tomorrow. Resolutely, he sets off for his castle to prepare for his own demise.

There, in his tower, Manfred is confronted by the two forces battling over all of humanity. The local abbot, on behalf of God, comes to urge Manfred to repent and seek forgiveness. He tries to reassure the magician that there is still time to find salvation, but Manfred rejects his offer, claiming that the judgment a man makes on himself is far more powerful and condemning than any divine one. His world has been desolation and despair, and he has lost hope of anything better.

Once Manfred rejects divine salvation, the minions of the Devil appear and try to claim him as theirs. With equal ferocity, Manfred rejects their demand for his soul as well. Because his powers came entirely from his own efforts, not from a bargain with demonic forces, he owes hell no debt; besides, he claims, his internal torment is far worse than any punishment hell could devise for him. The demons vanish, leaving the abbot one last chance to beg Manfred to repent, but again Manfred rejects him, choosing instead to die as he lived, alone.

Key Content Areas

Manfred is heavily influenced by the author's vision of the hero as a character whose independence is the source of his greatest strength. The Byronic hero is unconcerned with the values of society and answers only to himself, rising to power and fame through internal power rather than external approval. Manfred's struggle to balance his need for independence with the need for forgiveness is the driving force of the play; the character forces himself to find a resolution to his seemingly endless pain that he can accept. The result is a play that challenges readers to examine their values and beliefs and evaluate their own independence.

Potential Connections/Ideas

The plot of *Manfred* draws to some extent on the Faustus legend. Both Manfred and Faustus seek knowledge and obtain great magical power to understand their world and lives more clearly, but unlike Faustus, who receives his gifts from the Devil in exchange for his soul, Manfred discovers his magic on his own and owes no debts. Two fine versions of the Faustus story are available, Goethe's *Faust* and Marlowe's *The Tragic Tale of Doctor Faustus,* and either could be used side by side with *Manfred* to clarify the distinction between the morality endorsed through Faustus's punishment and the amoral nature of the Byronic hero.

　　　Teachers wishing to highlight the characteristics of a Byronic hero might turn to other literature featuring such heroes, such as Heathcliff in Emily Brontë's *Wuthering Heights* or Jerry Renault in Robert Cormier's *The Chocolate War.* Another possibility would be to consider the various types or models of heroes in literature, including the traditional hero of the heroic epic (Odysseus in *The Odyssey*), the tragic hero (Oedipus in *Oedipus Rex,* Hamlet in *Hamlet*), and the pathetic hero (Willy Loman in *Death of a Salesman*). Either comparison might begin with a discussion of the reasons we need heroes and end by considering what purposes each form of hero is best suited for.

　　　Finally, teachers might want to look closely at Byron's use of "dramatic poetry," examining the form and asking why the author would choose to write his poem in the form of a play, but one clearly not meant to be acted. What does Byron gain through his use of the dramatic form that he cannot get from poetry alone? Could the play be effectively produced in the modern theater? These questions might also lead to explorations of experimental drama, such as Sam Shepard's *Tongues* or any of Samuel Beckett's shorter works.

Red Flags

The ambiguous relationship between Manfred and Astarte might be interpreted as incestuous, but this is only one possible interpretation. Nothing in the play itself directly suggests that this is the case, and there is no other objectionable content.

Suggested Grade

The content of the play is suited to all grade levels and could be useful in the curriculum of almost any class. Ninth-graders could consider the differences between Manfred's fall and Oedipus' fall, and what role hubris plays in each drama. Tenth-graders could use Byron's stylized dramatic poetry as the European equivalent of "choreopoems" or sung dramas in African and Asian literature. Seniors could use *Manfred* as a benchmark of the rejection of religion for philosophy that sprang up among intellectuals following the Enlightenment.

Critical Readings

Stein, Atara. "'I loved her and destroyed her': Love and Narcissism in Byron's *Manfred*." *Philological Quarterly* 69, 2 (Spring 1990). 183–215. An excellent analysis of the character Manfred and Byron's effort to create a true romantic hero as paradoxically self-destructive. A lengthy, academic article, but worth the effort to read.

The Master Builder   *1892*

Henrik Ibsen

Characters: 4 Male; 3 Female
Leads: 3
Setting: The Solness house and the garden outside it
Length: Three acts

Synopsis

Halvard Solness, a master builder, bears a number of burdens. His marriage has been loveless since his home burned down years ago, and his wife suspects him of carrying on an affair with his secretary. He is, in fact, having the affair, but not out of love for Kaja. Instead, he maintains it to keep Kaja's fiancé, Ragnar, as an employee. Halvard feels that he is fighting off the advance of the younger generation, eventually destined to be pulled down just as Ragnar's father was by Halvard. To keep this from happening, Ragnar is carefully held in check by Halvard; nothing he does ever receives approval or endorsement. Ragnar's father pleads with Halvard to give his son a chance, so that he can move out on his own and marry Kaja, but Halvard refuses him.

In addition to his abilities, Halvard is also beginning to doubt his own sanity. He tells his wife's doctor that he has a strange power, as if things he wishes are made to come true by demons and spirits. His will becomes reality, and that has always been his strength, but he fears that if he lets anyone else take power away from him, he will lose control of the spirits. The doctor is baffled by this, but someone arrives who understands—Hilde, a young woman of twenty or so, who has been waiting for Halvard for the last ten years.

Hilde tells Halverd that when she was a child, at a celebration following one of Halvard's biggest successes, she watched him climb a church tower he had built to lay the wreath at the top. That evening, when he was feasting, Halvard promised Hilde he would come back for her in ten years and take her away to a castle he would build for her. Hilde took him seriously and has come to find the man who made such an impression on her. Halvard is at first shocked, but he is immediately drawn to Hilde's youth, beauty, and faith in him. At her urging, he approves Ragnar's plans, then dismisses the young man and Kaja as well. She is all he needs for his last project—a castle in the air he will build with her, for her. To prove he is capable of doing it, though, Hilde insists that he perform one last impossible feat for her. Halvard has been building a new home for his wife, with a huge tower at one end. Hilde asks Halvard to hang the capping wreath on the top of the tower, so she can see him standing like the master of all things once again. Halvard, seeing a chance to get back through Hilde something he lost years ago, agrees and mounts the scaffolding against doctor's orders, his wife's protests, and Ragnar's scoffing. He reaches the top of the tower and hangs the wreath, producing a frenzy of cheers from the crowd, but he loses his balance as he waves and then falls to his death. The curtain closes on the crowd in shock, and Hilde frantically cheering for her master builder.

Key Content Areas

The Master Builder focuses on the internal struggle of Halvard Solness. He is at once pleased with his power to control people's lives (he manipulates and orders around Kaja, Ragnar, and his wife with impunity and finds no resistance whatsoever) and disturbed by his inability to find happiness in doing so. Hilde's appearance is not only liberating for Halvard but also destructive; her demand that he fulfill his duty to her can be met only by his attempt to return to the joyous heights of his early career, when he was the younger generation overthrowing the old. Ironically, Hilde, a member of the younger generation that Halvard now fears, brings him to the top of his tower once again in a desperate effort to recapture his youth, but the attempt is nothing more than a castle built in the air, and the less hearty Halvard loses his balance and plunges to his death. Hilde's continued frenzied cheers for *her* master builder show us the reality that Halvard couldn't see—that Hilde is in love with her fantasy world, capable only of seeing the young man atop the world, not the older man living in fear of his inevitable overthrow.

Potential Connections/Ideas

The Master Builder is a play in which the main character refuses to confront the reality of his own aging; Halvard still sees himself as the master of his field, commanding supernatural forces to do his will. Like Willy Loman in Arthur Miller's *Death of a Salesman,* Halvard lives in his own world. Each believes himself still at the top of his career, and each believes he has done his duty as father and husband to the fullest extent. Neither sees the destructive effect he has on those around him until it is too late, and both die to preserve what remains of their dream world.

Like Halvard, Jay Gatsby also exerts a powerful magnetism over those in his wake, never fully considering the consequences. Fitzgerald's *The Great Gatsby* is an interesting work to compare with *The Master Builder;* Gatsby's casual dismissal of law and social order is done with the same carelessness that Halvard seduces Kaja or manipulates Ragnar to meet his needs. Both characters are destroyed by their own conviction that they are indestructible.

As a play with the focus mainly on the protagonist's struggle to recapture joy in his life, *The Master Builder* might also be compared or connected with works such as August Wilson's *Fences,* Kate Chopin's *The Awakening,* or Lillian Hellman's *Toys in the Attic.* Also worth considering for a potential contrast of the leading characters is Arthur Miller's *The Crucible;* John Proctor is another man whose magnetic power and forceful nature allow him to dominate many people but who forgets how to find love and joy after cheating on his wife. He is racked with guilt and acts only as a dutiful husband, pained to be even in the same room as his wife, until he is forced to confront his failings and given a chance to show his true spirit. Doing so frees him from the guilt he has suffered but brings his death in the process. Proctor, however, dies a hero; Halvard dies still pursuing his own vanity.

Red Flags

None.

Suggested Grade

The Master Builder is a difficult play to understand, though not hard to read. Seniors are most likely to grasp Halvard's struggle, though sophomores may be able to follow the action with some assistance from a teacher.

"Master Harold" . . . and the boys   *1982*

Athol Fugard

Characters: 3 Male; 0 Female
Leads: 3
Setting: A tearoom in Port Elizabeth, South Africa, 1950
Length: One act (but full length)

Synopsis

Two black men, Willie and Sam, are cleaning up the tearoom when the owner's son, Hally, arrives. Sam, we learn, has acted as a father figure for Hally, whose real father is an alcoholic in the hospital undergoing treatment. When Hally learns that his father is coming home that day, he isn't pleased. The three discuss their shared lives, times spent together as Hally grew up, and the things each taught the others. Hally seems at first to be a "child of hope"—someone raised in the apartheid system who despises racism. When Sam chides him, however, for joking about his father's drunkenness, Hally explodes angrily. The argument spirals until Hally demands that Sam call him "Master Harold," pointedly reminding him of the difference in their positions. Sam bitterly attacks Hally's behavior, warning him that he will never call Hally anything but "Master Harold" again if he is forced to do so once. The confrontation is defused at the close of the play when the two realize that they have both gone too far, but the damage seems to have been done, and the play ends with Hally trying to convince Sam and the audience that everything will be better tomorrow.

Key Content Areas

"Master Harold" . . . and the boys is a play about the forces that pull people apart. The context of the play, apartheid South Africa, only underscores this idea; the focus is not the setting but rather the dynamics, and the play could just as easily be set in the slavery era of American history. At the core of the text, Fugard seems to be disabusing us of the idea that children raised in a society where racism exists will avoid the taint from simply living alongside the minority. Hally grows up in the care of Willie and Sam and clearly has a much stronger love for Sam than for his own father, but neither fact prevents him from falling back into racism when he loses his temper.

Potential Connections/Ideas

Fugard's perspective on race relations is a natural fit with any other text that discusses life as a member of a minority culture. Sandra Cisneros's *The House on Mango Street* is one such book, as is Ralph Ellison's *Invisible Man. "Master Harold"* could also be used in tandem with Anna Deavere Smith's *Twilight: Los Angeles, 1992,* an account of the Los Angeles riots and the racial tensions that sparked them. Teachers wanting to bridge modern tensions with past issues might connect this play to Jane Austen's novel *Mansfield Park,* in which social position measures personal worth, or Dickens's *Great Expectations,* in which a poor boy falls in love with a wealthy girl but is considered an unsuitable match. *Huckleberry Finn* is another possible companion text, with students drawing comparisons between Jim and Huck's relationship and Hally and Sam's.

Red Flags

Many. There are several instances of profanity, and in one scene Sam drops his trousers and displays his backside. There are threats of beatings and discussions of canings. Still, the benefits of this well-written, thoughtful piece far outweigh these negatives and make it worth the extra effort to get permission slips or board approval.

Suggested Grade

This play is suitable for grades ten through twelve. Younger students may too quickly dismiss the material as "preachy." Older students should be able to discuss the prickly subject matter thoughtfully, particularly those who have already taken American history classes.

Film Versions

Master Harold . . . and the boys. Dir. Michael Lindsay-Hogg. With Matthew Broderick and Zakes Mokae. 1985. 90 min. (PG-13)

Critical Readings

Durbach, Errol. *"Master Harold" . . . and the boys:* Athol Fugard and the Psychology of Apartheid." *Modern Drama* 30 (Dec. 1987): 505-13. Explores the psychological construction in *Master Harold* of apartheid as something ingrained in daily life, beyond simple law, and the danger of dismissing the play as irrelevant following the end of apartheid laws.

Jordan, John O. "Life in the Theatre: Autobiography, Politics, and Romance in *"Master Harold" . . . and the boys. Twentieth Century Literature* 39 (Winter 1993): 461-72. Argues that Fugard's play is a romance, not a tragedy, best seen from the freedom Willie and Sam exercise to dance around the sullen racist incident involving Hally. The essay also notes the autobiographical influences in the play.

Measure for Measure

c. 1604

William Shakespeare

Characters: up to 18 Male; 6 Female
Leads: 5
Setting: Vienna, 1600s
Length: Five acts

Synopsis

The Duke, ruler of Vienna, decides to pretend to leave town in order to test Lord Angelo, whose apparently rigid morality the Duke has cause to doubt. He leaves Angelo in charge, then returns disguised as a friar to observe. Angelo immediately begins enforcing laws against immorality that have been previously ignored, and as a result Claudio is arrested for impregnating his betrothed, Julietta, and sentenced to death as an example. Claudio's sister, Isabella, who is about to enter a convent, is informed of Claudio's sentence and returns to plead for his life. Angelo, struck by Isabella's beauty and piety, offers her a choice—sleep with him and he will pardon Claudio, or refuse and let him die. Isabella, stunned, refuses his offer and resigns herself to Claudio's death. When she goes to tell her brother of her choice, however, he pleads with her to reconsider; angered by his cowardice, she storms out.

All seems lost, and Claudio's execution seems inevitable, but the Duke, still in disguise, intervenes and promises to help Isabella keep her honor and still save her brother. He introduces Isabella to Mariana, a woman whom Angelo pledged to marry but abandoned when her fortune was lost before the wedding. Mariana, still in love with Angelo, agrees to take Isabella's place in bed, and in the dark, Angelo falls for the ruse. After deceiving Angelo, Isabella confronts him publicly, accusing him of abusing his power. Faced with the Duke's condemnation, Angelo confesses but is forgiven by Isabella, who is reunited with Claudio. The Duke offers Isabella his hand in marriage as the play ends.

Key Content Areas

Measure for Measure deals with many issues, but the ones that resonate most with modern audiences are sexual harassment and the abuse of power. These two issues overshadow the questions of morality and piety that were probably the original center of the play, questions debated extensively between Angelo and Isabella in their meetings and explored in their soliloquies.

Potential Connections/Ideas

Measure for Measure has gained increasing popularity as a stage production in recent years, particularly in light of the attention sexual harassment is finally receiving in the United States. Teachers could draw students into the play by using historical events such as Anita Hill's claim of sexual harassment by Supreme Court nominee Clarence Thomas, which broaches the issues of gender and power involved in sexual harassment, using it as a bridge to the play. Alternatively, a class of juniors or seniors might begin by studying *Measure for Measure,* then move to David Mamet's *Oleanna,* in which the case is much less clear, and compare the two. Alternatively, Samuel Richardson's hugely popular eighteenth-century novel, *Pamela,* and Henry Fielding's scathing parody of the work, *Shamela,* could be added as part of a historical examination of the perspectives on sexual harassment over the centuries and where responsibility for such behavior is placed.

I have had particular success with *Measure for Measure* in the high school classroom by concentrating on the ending of the play and the range of choices open to the director. As it is unclear if Isabella accepts the Duke's offer of marriage, there is room for discussion of all possible outcomes, not to mention the wisdom of the Duke's decision to marry Angelo to Mariana, the woman he dishonored. Such discussions are often animated and lend themselves to interpretive reading exercises to further explore the material.

Red Flags

Discussions of sexual harassment or gender and power issues may strike some as too political a topic for the classroom, but in this context, it seems unlikely that anyone would object to discussions of Angelo's abuses.

Suggested Grade

Suitable for any grade that can handle frank discussions that include the word *sex* but probably best for older students, who may have seen or experienced sexual harassment or abuses of power themselves or committed such acts.

Critical Readings

Chambers, R. W. "Measure for Measure." *Shakespeare: The Comedies,* Ed. Kenneth Muir. Englewood Cliffs, NJ: Prentice Hall, 1965. 88–108. An impassioned defense of the play as moral and reasonable and the characters as redeemable.

Lawrence, William W. *Shakespeare's Problem Comedies.* New York: Unger, 1960. Contains an extended chapter covering the play and arguments regarding the morality of each character. A bit dated, having been first published in 1933, but still a very readable analysis.

Schanzer, Ernest. *The Problem Plays of Shakespeare.* New York: Schocken, 1963. The chapter on *Measure for Measure* takes the position that the play is neither a cynical indictment nor a Christian paean but rather an exploration of public and private ethics, examining the five main characters in particular.

Zender, Karl F. "Isabella's Choice." *Philological Quarterly* 73 (Winter 1994): 77–93. Solid discussion of the setup Shakespeare creates for *Measure for Measure* and the nonresolution of the play's conclusion.

The Monkey's Paw

1910

W. W. Jacobs and Louis N. Parker

Characters: 4 Male; 1 Female
Leads: 2
Setting: An old-fashioned English cottage
Length: One act (three scenes)

Synopsis

On a stormy night in the countryside, Sergeant-Major Morris comes to visit the White household. When the conversation turns to magic, the sergeant produces a strange object he received from a fakir while on his travels with the army—a shriveled monkey's paw. According to the sergeant, the magic paw can grant three wishes each to three people, but those who had the wishes granted would certainly regret them. Though the sergeant assures them the story is true and that he has had his three wishes and regretted them, the Whites are intrigued and skeptical. Against the sergeant's dire warnings, they keep the paw, and after he leaves, Mr. White wishes for the balance on his mortgage, two hundred pounds. Later that evening, his son, Herbert, dies in an accident at work. His company sends a messenger to the Whites, along with a check for two hundred pounds as a token of the company's sympathy. Convinced the paw is real, Mrs. White forces Mr. White to wish her son alive again. As he does, the house is plunged into darkness. Minutes later, a low knocking at the door begins, rising slowly to a thunderous pounding as Mrs. White struggles to get away from Mr. White, who is now terrified of what he has done and of what might be outside. As she desperately tries to open the door, he seizes the paw and, with the last wish, asks for his son to be returned to the grave at peace. Mrs. White flings open the door to find nothing but darkness beyond, and she swoons as the play ends.

Key Content Areas

The Monkey's Paw is an adapted horror story. It uses the "be careful what you wish for" trick that has appeared in many forms but is most notable for its use of melodramatic styling and heavy irony to create horror instead of the gore that movies often rely on.

Potential Connections/Ideas

The genre of the play, horror, immediately suggests that *The Monkey's Paw* would be well suited for use with works by Poe such as "The Fall of the House of Usher" and gothic novels such as Ann Radcliffe's *The Mysteries of Udolpho* or Mary Wollstonecraft Shelley's *Frankenstein* to illustrate the development of the genre. The "you'll regret your wish" motif could be taught alongside classical myths such as the stories of King Midas and Phaeton, the movie classic *It's a Wonderful Life,* or darker stories such as Washington Irving's "The Devil and Tom Walker" or Marlowe's *The Tragedy of Doctor Faustus.*

Red Flags

None. Nothing graphic occurs on stage, and there is a single use of the word *damned.*

Suggested Grade

This play is suitable for all high school students and quite easy to follow. It could be used to introduce irony to younger students, and its short length allows it to be easily combined into larger units for older students.

Film Versions

The Monkey's Paw. Dir. Norman Lee. 1948. B&W.
The Monkey's Paw. Dir. Wesley Ruggles and Ernest B. Schoedsack. 1932. B&W.

Mother Courage

Bertolt Brecht

Characters: 19 Male; 6 Female
Leads: 6–7
Setting: Sweden, 1624, and the following nine years of war
Length: Twelve scenes

Synopsis

Mother Courage spans nearly a decade of war and death in Sweden, Poland, and the countries between. "Mother Courage" is Anna Fierling, a woman who owns a trade wagon. When the play opens, Mother Courage is on her way to the front, hoping to sell her goods to the army, but instead she loses her two sons to a recruiter. She tells them that war is no honorable path and that the only way to find success in the world is to be content with being moderately successful and mostly happy. The lure of heroism seduces Eilif and Swiss Cheese, however, and they join up. Mother Courage and her mute daughter, Kattrin, forge onward, buying and selling as the war rages around them. They watch people growing hungrier and armies rising and falling in power, but Mother Courage always remains steadfastly focused on what's best for her (primarily) and her family. At one point, she talks about the importance of the war continuing; in peacetime, who will buy her goods? She even tries to negotiate when her son Swiss Cheese is captured by the enemy, and as a result he is executed. Despite this callousness, however, Brecht makes sure we cannot universally condemn Mother Courage. She refuses an offer of marriage and a profitable business when she learns that it doesn't include taking in her daughter, and she saves an angry young soldier's life by persuading him that injustice sometimes must be tolerated to survive. After Kattrin dies while trying to warn a village of an impending invasion, Mother Courage is left to push her way on alone, hurrying off to the front once again.

Key Content Areas

The focus of *Mother Courage* is not war or its validity; Brecht assumes that war is an incontrovertible fact. As one sergeant says, war brings order to nations falling into chaos and is therefore a necessity every so often. It is the question of how to survive in a world that operates by these rules that is at the center of *Mother Courage*. Is Mother Courage right to claim that cynicism is the only way to approach the world safely, or does it end up costing her more than anyone else? Brecht uses war as a way of questioning approaches to life.

Potential Connections/Ideas

Mother Courage's cynical point of view echoes the frustrations voiced in Molière's comedy *The Misanthrope*, or it could be compared with the cultivated cynicism of Jacques in Shakespeare's *As You Like It*. Other texts in which the leading character is "doing what must be done to survive" include *Going after Cacciato*, Tim O'Brien's story of the pursuit of a soldier gone AWOL during Vietnam, and *Moll Flanders*, Daniel Defoe's classic novel of a woman who falls into disrepute in eighteenth-century London. The question of supporting war and the responsibility of those who do so is also discussed in George Bernard Shaw's *Arms and the Man*. Historically, *Mother Courage* could be taught in conjunction with discussions of the industry of war or in discussions of social responsibility that go with modern issues such as AIDS and poverty.

Red Flags

Some foul language, but nothing that isn't used on network television today.

Suggested Grade

Best for upper grades. The behavior of the characters is simple enough to understand, in that it mimics much of the "me-first" attitude present in American society today. Discussions of personal responsibility and social responsibility, however, are often more complex and better left to students who have experienced such responsibility. With the growing number of students who balance school and work and the increasing portion of family responsibilities which they shoulder, students have more than ever to say on these questions.

Film Versions

Mother Courage. Dir. Peter Palitzsch and Manfred Weckwerth. 1960. B&W. (German)

The Mousetrap

1954

Agatha Christie

Characters: 5 Male; 3 Female
Leads: 8
Setting: An English manor house converted to an inn, present day
Length: Full play

Synopsis

The Mousetrap is a murder mystery. As the play opens, we learn that a young lady has been strangled and that Scotland Yard is on the lookout for the killer. Meanwhile, a young couple, Mollie and Giles Ralston, are preparing for the first guests at Monkswell Manor, their new inn. A terrible snowstorm is making travel impossible, so it becomes clear as the guests arrive that no one will be arriving or leaving anytime soon. In addition to the four scheduled guests, a fifth arrives as well, his car stuck in a nearby snowdrift.

The guests are already testy when the police call the inn and inform Mollie that Sergeant Trotter is on his way to the hotel. When the news gets out, the guests become even more agitated. Trotter arrives on skis and tries to call in, only to learn that the telephone lines have gone dead. We learn that the murderer has almost certainly come to Monkswell; a notebook found at the scene indicates he intends to kill two people there. Everyone denies a connection to the first murder, but within minutes, Mrs. Boyle, one of the guests, is strangled. We then learn that Boyle was a magistrate in a case involving the first victim.

Understandably, the remaining guests are on edge, and Trotter angrily grills them to find out what they aren't revealing about their connection to the first murder. No one comes forward, however, and when Trotter's skis disappear, he decides that he needs to take action. He gets everyone to agree to "re-create" the murder, but with everyone playing different parts. Once they all move to their places, Trotter calls Mollie back to the parlor—and pulls a revolver. He reveals that he is the murderer, seeking revenge on the people who let him suffer years ago, and that Mollie was a teacher to whom his brother appealed for help, but who never responded. As he moves to kill her, two other guests enter. One is the sister of "Trotter," Kathy, who persuades him to come upstairs and take a sedative. The second is the real police officer, who came in place of another guest in hopes of trapping the murderer. With the madman apprehended, the play concludes.

Key Content Areas

The Mousetrap is not a play with a higher purpose. It is crafted for suspense, with clues and red herrings liberally interspersed in the action. It is a fine example of a stage mystery.

Potential Connections/Ideas

As a mystery, *The Mousetrap* could be compared with any of Agatha Christie's many novels as a way of highlighting the differences in the construction of the two types of literature. Alternatively, short mysteries such as Arthur Conan Doyle's classic Sherlock Holmes stories are quick and easy to read and follow the model for a mystery precisely. They are rigidly logical, which makes them ideal for use in practicing analysis. I regularly teach the mystery as an introduction to logical thought and analysis, and then move on to job-related logic tasks such as scheduling and strategic planning. For a more historical approach, connect this play to early models for the mystery novel, such as the gothic works of Edgar Allan Poe, Washington Irving, Mary Wollstonecraft Shelley, or Ann Radcliffe.

Red Flags

None.

Suggested Grade

Suitable for all high school students.

Mrs. Warren's Profession

1896

George Bernard Shaw

Characters: 4 Male; 2 Female
Leads: 6
Setting: Two cottages in the English countryside and their surroundings; an office
Length: Four acts

Synopsis

Mrs. Warren's Profession opens with Miss Vivie Warren, a particularly hearty woman in her early twenties home from college and taking a holiday in the country. Her reading is interrupted by the arrival of Mr. Praed, a friend of her mother come to visit. From Praed we learn that Mrs. Warren is on her way and will soon put in an appearance; Vivie, who seems less than pleased about that, tells Praed that while she isn't sure what her mother does, she has suspicions. Praed dodges the question until Mrs. Warren arrives.

Mrs. Warren is a handsome woman, well dressed and confident. She arrives with Sir George Crofts, a wealthy London man of the town, whom Vivie assumes is her mother's paramour. He is actually her partner in a chain of brothels extending throughout Europe, a business Mrs. Warren started with money she obtained as a prostitute early in her life. Vivie, incidentally, has a paramour of her own, Frank Samuels. Frank is the son of the local rector, Reverend Samuels, and is quite charming but also quite poor, having wasted his inheritance before it even passes into his hands. He has hopes of marrying Vivie out of both affection and an interest in her excellent financial position.

Reverend Samuels comes by the Warren house to try to bring Frank back home, but when he meets Mrs. Warren, it is revealed that she is the same woman he tried to pay years ago to conceal the relationship they had when he was young. Mortified, the rector stumbles over his words for the next few moments but quickly objects when he learns of Frank's interest in marrying Vivie. Mrs. Warren also objects, as does Sir George, who points out that the young man has no money and no prospects and that while he is in his fifties, he's more than willing to settle all his money and holdings on a young wife like Vivie.

Vivie, unaware of the objections to Frank, confronts her mother that night when Mrs. Warren tries to intervene and direct her to live a certain way. She demands to know what right her mother has to do so, particularly when Mrs. Warren's own profession was so distasteful. Mrs. Warren, angered by what she perceives as ingratitude and insolence from someone who has never experienced deprivation, attacks Vivie with vehemence. She tells Vivie about the dreadful conditions that she faced and the lack of a living wage in any honest employment for women. Given her choices and her talents, prostitution was the most practical one, and it offered her freedom the other jobs could not. Vivie is surprised and impressed by her mother's strength and courage, and the two make up.

The next day, however, Sir George proposes to Vivie, and she rejects his offer. When he explains that he is her mother's benefactor, having invested in her "businesses" to make it possible for them to succeed, he hopes to overcome her objections; instead, Vivie acknowledges the shame of having used money from the whorehouses to become an educated and independent woman, but again she rejects the source. Angered, Crofts tells Vivie that he and her mother are still running the whorehouses and that the profits were too high for Mrs. Warren to stop just because she no longer needed money for food and lodging. He also informs Vivie that she is the daughter of Reverend Samuels, the product of his affair with Mrs. Warren, and thus half-sister to Frank. Vivie, disgusted, renounces her mother and Frank entirely and leaves at once for London to take an accounting job.

In the play's final scene, both Frank and Mrs. Warren pursue Vivie to London. Frank arrives first and tries to persuade Vivie that Crofts was lying, but Vivie tells him that she was planning to break off with him, anyway. When he protests, she finally breaks down and in hysterics, reveals her mother's profession to him as explanation of why she is rejecting him. Frank, suddenly understanding, accepts her decision, knowing he could never live on money gained from such a trade, and knowing that without that money he could never provide for Vivie. Mrs. Warren then arrives, and Vivie confronts her about her ongoing trade. She dismisses her mother from her life forever, acknowledging that Mrs. Warren treated her well but in the end it was the education that she received that forces her to break with the provider. Happy at last, Vivie plunges herself into her accounting work—an honest job with a good wage that allows her true independence—as the play closes.

Key Content Areas

Mrs. Warren's Profession is a play of social protest that shows remarkable insight. On the one hand, Shaw is condemning the capitalists and profiteers who make it impossible for a woman to earn a living wage without risking her life (one of Mrs. Warren's sisters dies of lead poisoning from her work in a paint factory) or turning to prostitution. On the other hand, Shaw equally condemns Mrs. Warren for continuing to profit from the debasement of young women after acquiring the money she needed for a reasonable and honest lifestyle. Mrs. Warren's excuse is that she loved working and making money, but Vivie's ability to do the same, given a fair start, and without harming others in the process, leaves her mother as morally bankrupt as Crofts, who gladly and without shame accepts his 35 percent profit, dismissing the moral issue as something that great men never consider.

Potential Connections/Ideas

The desire for a woman to be independent and the obstacles to that independence are at the heart of a number of works, including Zora Neale Hurston's *Their Eyes Were Watching God* and George Eliot's *Middlemarch*. George Gissing's *The Odd Women* is the story of five unwed women in the 1890s who try to find stability, both economic and emotional, in a world that sees unmarried women as oddities.

Shaw's play particularly shines as a social commentary, and teaching it from that perspective offers a number of possibilities for connection into the curriculum. Read in conjunction with *Invisible Man*, Ralph Ellison's novel about the social and economic barriers facing young black men, and with a play such as Clifford Odets's *Waiting for Lefty* or Charles Dickens's novel *Hard Times*, each examining the pressures and frustrations facing the working class, students will be introduced to the concept of literature as a force for social change. The controversial nature of such social commentary and the outrage it can draw might also be worth discussion; Shaw's "apology" for his play, in which he challenges the government decision that banned the play for its immorality for eight years, is a good starting place for such a discussion. From there, a unit on censorship and a community's right to set standards of decency is a logical step, offering rich potential for research and debate on banned books and the reasons for their censorship.

Red Flags

No sexual activity takes place at any point in the play, but the fact that Mrs. Warren is the owner and proprietress of several whorehouses and a former prostitute herself may prove too much for more conservative school districts. Although school board members and administrators who read the play will almost certainly realize that Shaw is condemning Mrs. Warren and her lack of morals, teachers are strongly cautioned to have this play reviewed and approved for use by a principal to avoid controversy. In this case, Shaw's play is worth the extra effort needed to teach it.

Suggested Grade

Because of the subject matter and the necessity of taking Mrs. Warren's arguments seriously for the play's point to be understood, this text should be taught only to seniors and, if necessary, only to advanced or honors classes. A mature group of students who are willing to consider the play carefully may find that Mrs. Warren's frustration at finding a job that pays a living wage is similar to that of students who drop out of high school or try to find employment with a high school diploma alone.

Film Versions

Mrs. Warren's Profession. 1972. UK television production.

Critical Readings

Morgan, Margery M. *The Shavian Playground.* London: Methuen, 1972. 36–45. A short discussion of the way Shaw lures the audience into supporting Mrs. Warren despite her "socially unacceptable" position.

Valency, Maurice. *The Cart and the Trumpet: The Plays of George Bernard Shaw.* New York: Oxford University P, 1973. 92–101. Focuses on the strengths of *Mrs. Warren's Profession* (its social analysis) and its weaknesses (Vivie's lack of character development.)

My Children! My Africa! $\qquad$ *1989*

Athol Fugard

Characters: 2 Male; 1 Female
Leads: 3
Setting: A small town in Cape Karoo, South Africa, autumn 1984
Length: Full play

Synopsis

Fugard's play opens in the midst of a debate between Thami Mbikwana, a black student in his final year of high school, and Isabel Dyson, a white student from a neighboring school. Isabel has been invited to come and debate at Thami's school, and accepted, thinking it would be a great opportunity to help the underprivileged black students. What she thinks she finds is a group of people who treat her as an equal, judging her on her words and nothing else. Finding that she is expected to prove herself, she argues passionately against the popular Thami, and defeats him in a narrow vote.

After the debate, Thami and Isabel talk and get to know each other. Both have won each other's respect and admiration in the debate, and their conversation borders on flirtatious. Thami's teacher, Mr. Myalatya (who everyone calls Mr. M) is equally impressed by the debate and pleased that Isabel is excited by his class instead of intimidated by the stares and cool reception. He sees how well she and Thami get along and invites the two of them to compete as a team in the upcoming English literature contest, and she eagerly accepts.

As the contest approaches, however, trouble looms. Isabel and Mr. M can see a clear change in Thami, who is becoming progressively more distant. When Isabel confronts him about it, Thami explains that there are troubles bigger than an English competition and that big changes are coming. Revolution is in the air, and Thami, educated enough to know that he can never take advantage of his education under the current system, is in the heart of it. Isabel asks why Thami is rejecting everything Mr. M taught him about the importance of education in changing the world; Thami replies that Mr. M is part of the problem as a teacher who preaches slow, nonviolent change. He tells Isabel that he is pulling out of the competition, and when Mr. M confronts him about his revolutionary friends and their ideas, Thami tells his teacher that the school is going to be boycotted and that many are suggesting that Mr. M is an informer who should be dealt with accordingly. He warns the teacher not to be at the school when the boycott starts.

Mr. M refuses to listen and defies the boycott. His ringing of the school bell draws an angry crowd. Thami comes in to try to talk him out of what he is doing, but Mr. M will not be swayed. Angered by the desertion of his favorite pupil, the one he had pinned his hopes on, Mr. M tells Thami that he also reported the names of all the lead demonstrators to the police. He regrets it but knows that Thami can never forgive him for the betrayal and believes that he has lost his hoped-for world. With nothing left to live for, he continues to ring the school bell, going out to confront the crowd, which kills him brutally.

Isabel and Thami meet once more, as Thami is fleeing to the north to escape the police. Isabel demands an explanation of what has happened and insists on knowing what sort of a revolution for equality prevents a white and a black from being seen together as friends. In the end, however, it becomes clear that while she and Thami can get along as equals, their worlds cannot. Thami flees the country to continue his fight as a rebel; Isabel, left behind, vows to carry on Mr. M's fight from the inside.

Key Content Areas

Racial tension in smoldering South Africa is a large part of the context of this play, but Fugard's drama probes below the surface of this conflict to question how individual bonds can be expanded into community relations. The question of radical movements and "freedom at any cost" is also considered.

Potential Connections/Ideas

My Children! My Africa! is a powerful play, loaded with tension and confrontation. Most frustrating is the sense that the viewer gets that what Isabel and Thami find is the real connection and honest friendship between equals that is so sought after in our divided society, but in that event that rare success turns out to be too weak to overcome an entire community. We are given cause to hope for racial reconciliation and then find it dragged away from us. Fugard's challenge to the oft-promoted notion that open-mindedness can overcome racism will likely produce strong reactions from students and offers a great opportunity for further discussion and exploration. For teachers interested in exploring this question, the text is perhaps best paired with another Fugard play, *"Master Harold" . . . and the boys*, which looks at the community forces that tear apart blacks and whites who have a long history of friendship and love.

Fugard's plays have drawn a fair amount of criticism, particularly from those who feel that his works on South African conflict encourage blacks to accept slow change instead of taking an aggressive approach to bringing an end to apartheid. (See the essay by Nicholas Visser for a complete discussion.) To ignore the issues surrounding Fugard, a white playwright producing ostensibly antiapartheid dramas but using black characters to voice an opposition to aggressive political activism, would be inappropriate, and some effort should be made to address these issues in class.

Other texts that might be used in conjunction with Fugard's play include Anna Deavere Smith's *Fires in the Mirror*, which looks at ethnic conflict between Jews and African Americans in Crown Heights, New York, which resulted in rioting in 1991. Teachers looking for texts with parallels to the internal community conflict represented by Mr. M and Thami should consider works such as Toni Morrison's *Song of*

Solomon, Harriet Beecher Stowe's *Uncle Tom's Cabin,* Wole Soyinka's *Death and the King's Horseman,* or Sean O'Casey's *Juno and the Paycock,* each of which explores the pressures an oppressed community puts on individual members to conform at all costs—pressures that often exceed those of the oppressors.

Red Flags

Three uses of profanity. The lines are editable, but a significant amount of passion in a key scene would be lost by their absence.

Suggested Grade

For seniors and advanced juniors. Fugard's worldview is a depressing one; his argument against the strength of individuals in overcoming racial hostility is potentially frustrating for today's students, who strongly believe they can avoid their parents' mistakes. Discussions of Thami's choices and their propriety could become heated and should be carefully moderated, particularly if people begin turning to personal experiences for discussion examples.

Critical Readings

Visser, Nicholas. "Drama and Politics in a State of Emergency: Athol Fugard's *My Children! My Africa!*" *Twentieth Century Literature* 39 (Winter 1993): 486–502. Points out the problematic, semi-revisionist position Fugard takes in the play and condemns the text as propaganda to salve the white liberal masses of South Africa.

Oedipus Rex

c. 425 B.C.

Sophocles

Characters: 5–7+ Male; 1–3+ Female
Leads: 5
Setting: The palace of Oedipus, king of Thebes
Length: Roughly five acts

Synopsis

Oedipus Rex opens with a chorus gathered at the palace of Oedipus, begging for his help in finding a cure for the plague that seems to have struck the city. Oedipus answers that he has already sent his father-in-law, Creon, to find the source of the problem. Creon informs the crowd that the oracle has revealed that Laius, the previous king of Thebes, was murdered and never avenged and that the plague will continue until the murderer is brought to justice. Oedipus swears that he will bring the plague to an end himself by finding the murderer and boldly calls down terrible curses on the traitor.

When no one comes forward to take blame for the murder, Tiresias, the blind seer, is called in to help identify the killer. He is very evasive, however, and finally flatly refuses to tell who the murderer is. This enrages Oedipus, who accuses him of plotting the murder himself. Tiresias, in turn, is outraged, and he reveals that it is Oedipus who is the source of the plague. Oedipus, of course, is shocked and immediately dismisses Tiresias's words as nonsense and treason, but he cannot avoid the truth. First, we learn that Laius was murdered in a foreign land. We learn that his son was supposed to murder him, but to avoid this, Laius had him left as a baby on a mountainside with his ankles bolted together.

Oedipus at once recognizes details of his own birth and of the encounter he had on the road to Thebes before meeting the Sphinx. He realizes that he is indeed the murderer of his father and now the husband of his mother. Horrified by his actions, however unknowing, Oedipus's wife, Jocasta, hangs herself, and her husband puts out his own eyes. He is left to wander, an outcast condemned by his own rash words as king.

Key Content Areas

Oedipus is a classic Greek tragedy and ideal for illustrating this very formal style. Its focus is on hubris, or excessive pride, and the results of that pride. Oedipus's flaw isn't the unfortunate circumstances in which he finds himself; it is his unwillingness to listen and his self-aggrandizing boasts that bring about his fall from grace.

Potential Connections/Ideas

Oedipus is one of the prime examples of a story centering on a hero with a tragic flaw. Other stories built on or around this theme include Shakespeare's *Othello*, Miller's *Death of a Salesman*, and Fitzgerald's *The Great Gatsby*. *Oedipus* could also be taught as part of a discussion of the history of the theater, with attention paid to the development of the chorus into supporting cast, the construction of the amphitheater, and the replacement of a rigid form with a flexible structure as time passes. It could also be compared to Greek comedies, such as Aristophanes' *The Birds*, to give students an idea of the two extremes of Greek drama.

Red Flags

At the heart of the story is a hero who kills his father, sleeps with his mother, and then has two children by her. Despite the profound historical importance of this play, this content may be objectionable to some school systems.

Suggested Grade

Best for tenth grade and up. Probably more suited to older students, but the benefits of familiarizing students with the roots of drama early on makes worthwhile the additional effort needed to teach a difficult piece.

Film Versions

Oedipus Rex. Dir. Tyrone Guthrie. With Douglas Rain, Douglas Campbell. 1957. 87 min. (NR)

Oedipus the King. Dir. Phillip Saville. 1968. 97 min. (NR)

Oedipus Rex. Dir. Don Taylor. 1984. UK TV version. 111 min.

Patience

1881

W. S. Gilbert and Sir Arthur Sullivan

Characters: 6 (plus chorus) Male; 5 (plus chorus) Female
Leads: 10
Setting: Pastoral glades and Castle Bunthorne (a country estate), 1881
Length: Two acts

Synopsis

The eligible women of the town have all fallen in love with an "aesthetic" poet named Reginald Bunthorne but despair of success in wooing him because he has fallen madly in love with Patience, the town's milkmaid, and the only woman who doesn't like Bunthorne in the slightest. Patience is in love with Archibald Grosvenor, her former nursery mate and now a "fleshy" poet of handsome figure. Grosvenor is known as "Archibald the All-Right" because he is perfect in every way, and he confidently asks Patience to marry him, but she refuses. In her search for information on love, Patience has learned that she should be seeking a selfless love and that a love that is desired must hence be unacceptable.

Meanwhile, the local Dragoon Guards who have returned to visit their former flames find that the young ladies have deserted them for Bunthorne, and they are highly displeased. Bunthorne, long spurned by Patience, decides to offer himself to one of his admirers as a prize in a lottery, and tickets sell quickly over the protests of the Dragoons. Just as the drawing is about to take place, Patience interrupts. Having learned that the only true love is a love entirely unrelated to one's own happiness, she offers to take Bunthorne as husband because she despises him. He quickly accepts.

Bunthorne's admirers are ready to return to the Dragoon Guards, now that their idol is committed to marry, but just as the lovers are reuniting, Grosvenor appears on the scene, heartbroken at Patience's refusal of his suit. To his dismay (and that of the Dragoons, who are dumped again!), the young ladies instantly fall for him. Bunthorne, long accustomed to constant admiration, finds himself alone and unappreciated. Angered, he forces Grosvenor, under threat of a curse, to drop his poetic pose and become "common" in manner, and Grosvenor, tired of being perfect and hounded by admirers, agrees to let Bunthorne take on his style. As a result, Bunthorne becomes perfect; Patience, however, leaves him for the now-imperfect Grosvenor, and the women, following Grosvenor's perfect judgment, become average in style and consent to marry the Dragoons, leaving only Bunthorne without a wife as the play ends.

Key Content Areas

Patience is arguably Gilbert and Sullivan's best satiric (or parodic, depending on your point of view) work. It mocks the English craze for the aesthetic poetry of authors like Wilde and Swinburne, as well as the odd attire and pretentious dispositions that these and other "aesthetic artists" put on at the time.

Potential Connections/Ideas

Perhaps the best way to work with *Patience* is by presenting it in the company of the work it is ridiculing. Paired, for example, with the poetry of Swinburne or the odd, posing characters of Wilde's *The Importance of Being Earnest,* the play's commentary and sarcasm seem less fantastic and more realistic. Comparisons of the character of Bunthorne and his poetry and that of Wilde and his works invite questions regarding the fairness of Gilbert's criticism. Was Wilde an "aesthetic sham"? An alternative path to integrating *Patience* into the classroom is to use it as a bridge from the idea of parody itself to larger works as parody. Moving from poetry units that utilize parody as a writing prompt to close examinations of the poetic parody within *Patience* would be one such bridge. The opera could also be used as a bridge to a historical study of the aesthetic movement or as part of a unit on the way society tends to follow fads from time to time, even if it is aware that the fads are silly.

Red Flags

None. Gilbert was an extreme moralist, and his plays are as rigid as Victorian morality can make them.

Suggested Grade

The vocabulary needed to follow some portions of the play and the historical and cultural references involved may make it too hard for younger students to understand beyond the surface comedy. Older students, however, should appreciate it, and the music is particularly enjoyable. Best for eleventh and twelfth grades.

Film Versions

Patience. Dir. John Cox and Cameron Kirkpatrick. 1995.

The Physicists

1962

Friedrich Dürrenmatt

Characters: 13–15 Male; 4 (+1 dead body) Female
Leads: 5
Setting: A private sanatorium somewhere in Western Europe,
   likely Switzerland, 1960s
Length: Two acts

Synopsis

The Physicists opens with the dead body of a nurse center stage and the arrival of the police to investigate. We quickly learn of the three interesting patients housed at this facility: one who believes himself to be Einstein, one who thinks he's Newton, and one who speaks with King Solomon. Coincidentally, all three men are physicists. As the play progresses, however, we learn that nobody in the play is entirely who they appear to be. Johann Wilhelm Möbius merely pretends to speak to Solomon to hide his terrible secret—the newly discovered principle of universal discovery, the basic equation underlying the entirety of physics, and a potential engine of devastation. The other two "madmen" are revealed to be secret agents seeking Möbius's theory who have entered the madhouse to find him. After the three debate, they agree that the danger of the secret escaping is too great and that they must remain confined in the madhouse for the rest of their lives. Just when the play appears over, however, one last terrible twist remains. The owner of the asylum has been watching Möbius closely and has secretly duplicated the papers he destroyed. Using the principle of universal discovery, she has built an industrial empire that has begun the process of global domination, and the only ones who could warn the world—the physicists who hoped their scientific principles would be enough to keep the genie in the bottle—are hopelessly imprisoned for life inside the asylum, a prison they created for themselves.

Key Content Areas

Writing just after the discovery of the potential for atomic warfare, Dürrenmatt was highly interested in the ethical aspects of science and how knowledge discovered can never be kept truly apolitical or exist "for knowledge's sake." Consequently, *The Physicists* is somewhat political and somewhat ethical in focus, but it could be used in discussions of war, scientific ethics, and the question, "Is it always best to seek to know everything?"

Potential Connections/Ideas

Where the ethical questions of *Macbeth* or *Hamlet* are considered, one could easily use *The Physicists* in their place. I think this is a fantastic play, with many, many levels that can be explored. Who commits the worse crimes, the physicists who murder to (they think) save humanity, or those who use their work for evil purposes? Can we hold anyone responsible for the moral dimension of science? How? When do we do the right thing, and how do we decide what the right thing is?

As a play set firmly in the cold war era, the potential for cross-disciplinary linkage is high. One could turn to nonfictional accounts of Oppenheimer's research on the atomic bomb or to history texts for a discussion of the mentality of America during the arms race. A debate on the pros and cons of the nuclear age (does nuclear energy as a resource offset the potential threat of nuclear war?) might prove engrossing and educational, as well as emotional.

Finally, Dürrenmatt himself placed a list of twenty-one points he felt crucial to understanding *The Physicists* at the end of his play. Some of these points are complicated and hard to understand, but they are well worth the discussion time needed to untangle and explore them.

Red Flags

This is a modern morality play of sorts, and as such there is little offensive material. There is a violent strangulation scene on stage, and a nurse who says, "I want to sleep with you" to one of the patients.

Suggested Grade

The Physicists is suitable for anyone mature enough to sit through its occasional long stretches. The action should make sense to nearly any high school student, but I would recommend it for grades nine and up because of the history involved.

Critical Readings

Dürrenmatt, Friedrich. "A Monster Lecture on Justice and Law." *Friedrich Dürrenmatt: Plays and Essays.* Ed. Volkmar Sandler. New York: Continuum, 1982. 263–312. A lecture in which Dürrenmatt tells several stories that illuminate his political and social ideas.

Reno, Robert P. "Science and Prophets in Dürrenmatt's *The Physicists.*" *Renascence* 37.2 (Winter 1985): 70–79. A discussion of the construct Möbius uses to try to protect his powerful discoveries and the biblical metaphor of King Solomon, which Dürrenmatt uses to show he has erred dangerously.

Picnic

1953

William Inge

Characters: 4 Male; 6 Female
Leads: 7
Setting: A small town in Kansas, in the yards of the Owens's and Potts's houses.
Length: Full play

Synopsis

In *Picnic,* two sisters, Madge and Millie Owens, take center stage. Madge is "the pretty one," the one who gets all the compliments, but who looks in a mirror just to prove to herself that she's really there. Her younger sister Millie is "the smart one," and she resents Madge being the center of attention and popularity. The two have plans to go swimming that morning with Madge's boyfriend, Alan Seymour, a cultivated college boy. Flo, Millie and Madge's mother, hopes that the two will be married soon, and Alan gives us reason to believe that those hopes are valid.

When Alan comes to pick up Madge and Millie, he runs into Hal, a former college buddy who is working for his breakfast from Helen Potts, the Owens's next-door neighbor. Hal and Alan quickly begin to reminisce, and Alan invites him to join the party. Flo is not pleased, but she accepts Alan's friend for the sake of keeping alive her hopes for Madge's marriage.

Hal impresses both Millie and Madge from the start, and he is invited to be Millie's date at an evening picnic that night. As everyone is preparing for the party, Millie comes out looking radiant in a dress. For the first time, we see that she is as lovely as her sister. Madge, perhaps threatened by her sister's new blossoming, delays the party as she gets dressed. During the delay, however, a bottle of whiskey is produced by a neighbor, there are dancing and drinking on the front porch, and Millie gets sick. Hal is unjustly blamed for the mess and is berated by a drunken friend of the Owens's for being a no-good bum. The rest of the party heads to the picnic, leaving him to follow in his own car. Instead, Madge, who was to come later with the neighbors, comes out to talk with him, upset at the way he was treated. She and Hal quickly develop chemistry, and the two head off in his car, but not to the picnic.

Alan discovers what has happened and assumes that Madge was taken against her will, as she spends the next morning in tears. He and his father swear out warrants against Hal for auto theft, and Hal hides, looking for a chance to say good-bye to Madge. Finally, he sees an opportunity, and he confronts Madge, asking her if she loves him. When Madge doesn't reply, he asks her to come with him to Tampa, then takes off when she appears to refuse. Rejected by Madge, Alan also leaves, apparently for good. Flo is left to wonder where she went wrong with her daughter, until Madge comes out, suitcase in hand, and declares she's leaving for Tampa, chasing the one man she's met who made her tremble. As the curtain falls, Flo realizes how much she's missed that very feeling, and she can't bring herself to stop Madge.

Key Content Areas

Picnic is about love and what makes two people ideal for one another. Social status and money are often considerations, but Inge's play argues that none of that can replace the feeling when two people fall in love, and that people will willingly throw over everything else for the sake of love, even their values and their senses. It should be noted, however, that Inge uses fairly stereotypical characters of the 1950s to set his scene, and teachers may wish to discuss the sexist nature of *Picnic*'s conflicts.

Potential Connections/Ideas

The story of a stranger coming and winning the heart of a woman already promised to another is an old one, and many texts share this plot with *Picnic*. In the Renaissance, Shakespeare's *Romeo and Juliet* follows much the same story line (with more tragic results, of course). In the eighteenth century, dramas such as Centlivre's *A Bold Stroke for a Wife* and novels such as Jane Austen's *Sense and Sensibility* argue for the importance of like-minded individuals and suitable temperaments in marriage. In George Eliot's novel *Middlemarch*, Dorothea Brooke is forced to choose between her fortune and her love, penniless Will Ladislaw, and she chooses Ladislaw. Pip struggles to understand how his love for a beautiful heiress cannot overcome his lack of status and money in Dickens's *Great Expectations*. Finally, in F. Scott Fitzgerald's classic novel, *The Great Gatsby,* Gatsby struggles to keep his hold on Daisy, the woman he loves, but who he cannot understand wanted more than Gatsby's empty social shell.

Red Flags

A passing reference to an alteration made to a nude male statue by the local school board, and a sixteen-year-old girl drinks whiskey on stage and gets ill.

Suggested Grade

Ideal for eleventh- and twelfth-graders, most of whom will be actively dating or recently in a relationship and will have their own strong opinions on proper relationships and romance.

Film Versions

Picnic. Dir. Joshua Logan. With Kim Novak and William Holden. Columbia, 1956. 115 min.

Picnic. Remake of the Joshua Logan version. With Gregory Harrison and Jennifer Jason Leigh. Showtime, 1986.

Critical Readings

Shuman, R. Baird. *William Inge* (Rev. Ed.). Boston: Twayne, 1989. 263–312. A general thematic and character overview of *Picnic.*

The Playboy of the Western World   *1907*

J. M. Synge

Characters: 7+ Male; 5+ Female
Leads: 5
Setting: A shabby pub in the Irish countryside
Length: Three acts

Synopsis

The Playboy of the Western World begins with the beautiful and unruly barmaid, nick-named Pegeen Mike, speaking with her husband-to-be, Shawn Keogh, as she cleans up her father's pub. Shawn is a fat, pale farmer who is clearly beneath Pegeen in spirit; her father and the other regular customers are off to a wake, and when Pegeen asks Shawn to stay with her and keep her safe, Shawn is too cowardly to do so, arguing that the local priest, Father Reilly, would look ill upon a couple alone together at night before marriage.

Shawn quickly returns after leaving, however, frightened by a strange man in a nearby ditch. The man is Christy Mahon, and he hints that he is on the run from the police for having killed his father. His good looks and his story interest the group, particularly Pegeen Mike, who has her father take Christy on as a potboy for the pub. The men set off for the wake, leaving Christy and Pegeen behind. Shawn, now fearing he is about to lose his bride, offers to stay, but Pegeen throws him out, and the Widow Quin, whom he sends up later, as well.

The next morning, Christy finds that word of his arrival and his crime has spread. Three local girls come bringing him gifts, and the Widow Quin returns to try to catch him. Pegeen rebukes them, and Christy as well, but his protestations of affection for her calm her quickly.

Shawn and the widow return a few minutes later, catching Christy alone. Shawn offers Christy a bribe of fine clothing to leave town, but Christy refuses—things are going too well for him there. Of course, no sooner does he say this than his father, Old Mahon, appears, his head bandaged from the blow he took, but very much alive and hunting for his no-good son. The Widow Quin tries to use Mahon as blackmail to get Christy to marry her, but when she sees he has set his hopes on Pegeen Mike alone, she agrees to try to help him in exchange for a bribe of her own. The two decide to swear that Mahon is a madman and that his story is just ravings. The immediate problem settled, Christy is taken away by the girls to the town fair and the contests being held that day.

Bolstered with his newfound respectable character, Christy wins every contest. He is heralded as the "playboy of the western world," or the greatest athlete alive, and loaded with prizes. Flushed with victory, Christy asks Pegeen to marry him, and she agrees. Her father returns from the wake, accompanied by Shawn, who has finally received the marriage license the priest insisted on. Pegeen refuses to marry him, however, and when Shawn flees rather than fight Christy for her hand, her father gives them his blessing.

Mahon arrives again, angrier than ever, and begins beating Christy. Immediately, the town turns on Christy, who goes from respectable murderer to a no-good lying fool who pretended to kill his father to impress everyone. Unable to bear the reversal and facing a return to the terrible life he had before, Christy grabs a shovel and chases his father out, again striking him on the head and apparently killing him. He then returns to the pub, thinking that the town will once again regard him as a hero. Instead, the men slip a noose around his neck and try to pull him to the police, afraid that they will be implicated in the old man's death. Christy begs for help from Pegeen, but she attacks him as well, cursing him for a liar and a murderer. As they break Christy free from his hold on the table and begin to carry him off, Old Mahon staggers in again, reeling from the second blow, but still very much alive. Mahon lays into the men for daring to try to hang his son, and he quickly unties the boy, but Christy has found a new daring after the events of the day, and he tells his father that from now on, he's the one in charge. Mahon, shocked, acquiesces, and the two leave, Christy crowing that everything will fall right for him from now on. As the curtain falls, Pegeen falls to the floor, weeping, realizing that she has lost the one real man she ever met.

Key Content Areas

The Playboy of the Western World is a comedy, albeit a black one. If there's any message at its core, it would be that fortune favors the bold. Christy's meteoric rise, based only on his apparent murder of his father, is a comment on the public's tastes as well. Neither message is presented with a straight face, however, and the result is that we see how vital a hero is to a community barely surviving, where the promise of drinking for a day-long wake is the best escape possible, and to what length the people of that community are willing to go to find that hero and liven up their lives. Pegeen's loss is not of a man, but of her hopes for something better, something romantic, and it utterly crushes her.

Potential Connections/Ideas

Synge's play is perhaps best used as part of a broader look at Irish writing. Combined with James Joyce's *A Portrait of the Artist as a Young Man* or *Dubliners*, Brian Friel's *Translations*, and a selection of the poems of W. B. Yeats, *Playboy of the Western World* provides a view of the frustrations and hopes of the Irish as they struggle under British rule. Such a unit would be ideal as part of a broader exploration of English colonialism, including British rule in India (Forster's *A Passage to India*) and Africa (Wole Soyinka's *Death and the King's Horseman*). The perspective of the subject culture is illuminating and forces students to confront the fact that history is written by the victors.

Teachers looking to integrate *The Playboy of the Western World* into an existing curriculum have options as well. The transformation of a meek man to a confident hero-figure through a change of circumstances is similar to the change Celie undergoes in Alice Walker's novel *The Color Purple.* Henry, the young protagonist in Stephen Crane's *The Red Badge of Courage,* is much like Christy as well, beginning the story without any certainty or strength of character but, after confronting his own failures and weaknesses, refusing to return to them and taking the second chance he is offered by fate. Teachers might also use Synge's play to discuss the idea of socially constructed identity, an important issue in all of Jane Austen's novels, in Ralph Ellison's *Invisible Man,* in Virginia Woolf's *Mrs. Dalloway,* and in Hawthorne's *The Scarlet Letter.*

Red Flags

The Widow Quin is accused of freely taking lovers, but otherwise, nothing arises that might be offensive. Interestingly, this play sparked riots when first presented because crowds were outraged at the suggestion that Irish peasants would countenance a murderer and by one line in the play in which Christy suggests that not all the women of the town standing before him in their underwear would lure him away from Pegeen Mike. Times have certainly changed.

Suggested Grade

Suitable for all high school students. Synge's comedy is entertaining and moves along at a quick enough pace that younger students will not lose interest, yet contains enough material for discussion in the characters of Christy and Pegeen Mike that it remains meaningful for use with seniors.

Film Versions

The Playboy of the Western World. Dir. Brian Desmond Hurst. 1962. UK production.

The Playboy of the Western World. 1985. 118 min. (PG-13)

Critical Readings

Gerstenberger, Donna. *John Millington Synge.* New York: Twayne, 1964. 75–93. Discusses the development of Christy and Pegeen, including an explanation of the public riots at early performances of the play. Includes quotes from George Bernard Shaw on Synge's stereotyped Irishman.

Grene, Nicholas. *Synge: A Critical Study of the Plays.* Totowa, NJ: Rowman and Littlefield, 1975. 132–45. A general critical discussion of Christy's origins, character, and the general nature of the comedy as applied to Irish drama.

Price, Alan F. *Synge and Anglo–Irish Drama.* New York: Russell and Russell, 1972. 161–80. An overview of *The Playboy of the Western World* and the awakening of Christy to the imaginary self he creates.

Skelton, Robin. *J. M. Synge.* Cranbury, NJ: Associated University Presses, 1972. 57–70. A general discussion of Christian allegory in *The Playboy of the Western World* and the theme of rejection of the lover–hero.

Pygmalion

George Bernard Shaw

Characters: 4–6 Male; 6–8 Female
Leads: 5
Setting: London, 1913 or thereabouts
Length: Five acts

Synopsis

Henry Higgins, a phonetics professor, is sheltering himself from a sudden downpour when he overhears a flower girl speaking to a gentleman in a thick Cockney accent. Always interested in dialects, he writes down the colorful language she uses, only to be mistaken for an undercover police officer looking for prostitutes. In the uproar that ensues, we learn about Henry's skill at identifying a person's birthplace from their accent, and we learn that the gentleman in question, Colonel Pickering, was on his way to introduce himself to Henry as a fellow dialect enthusiast. The two head off, leaving a distraught and confused flower seller behind.

The next day, Eliza, the flower seller, appears at Henry's door, asking for language lessons. She hopes to work in a flower shop and thinks that elegant speech will help her get a job. Henry is amused by her presumption and is on the verge of throwing her out when the challenge of transforming Eliza into a lady sinks in. Certain of his abilities, Henry bets Pickering that he can pass Eliza off as a duchess within six months. Before she knows what is happening, Eliza is whisked away by a disapproving housekeeper for her first bath ever and a new set of clothes.

Henry and Pickering spend the next months teaching Eliza speech and manners, but they do so with a casual ignorance of what the changes will do to her. The two assume that when the bet is won or lost, Eliza will take her new skills and go off into the world somewhere; it simply isn't their concern. This lack of foresight isn't lost on the ladies in Henry's life—his housekeeper, his mother, and (of course) Eliza.

In due time, Henry and Pickering take Eliza on a practice outing, where she meets a young man named Freddy, who immediately falls in love with her. The test is a partial success; Eliza speaks marvelously but falls into the wrong sorts of conversational topics and occasionally swears impressively. Still, buoyed by their success, Pickering and Henry redouble their efforts. The big night rolls around, and they take Eliza to a full-scale social event. She performs magnificently, impressing everyone and prompting the hostess to scoff at the suggestion that she might be anything less than a princess quietly touring England.

The bet won, the trio return to Henry's house, but the two men, engrossed in the success of the evening and pleased to be done with the six-month experiment, utterly ignore Eliza's feelings as they talk about moving on to other things. She storms off, and agrees to marry Freddy. In the final scene of the play, she and Henry confront each other once again, and each comes to understand that while they will never be completely satisfied with the Pygmalion and Galatea relationship they have, they both care about each other and will remain a part of each other's lives.

Key Content Areas

In his introduction to the play, Shaw adamantly declares the play an effort to give England the hero it needs—a phonetics instructor capable of bringing the entire country to heel. He also claims the play is intentionally as didactic as possible in its style, presumably to get the need for a phonetics instructor across to the audience as clearly as possible. In addition to these openly avowed intentions, however, *Pygmalion* is also an investigation of the relationship between art and artist, and it indirectly serves as a commentary on the slippage between the carefully logical world of the academic and the emotional nature of the world the remainder of us inhabit.

Potential Connections/Ideas

The clearest connection to be made to *Pygmalion* is with the Greek myth from which the title is drawn, "Pygmalion and Galatea." Reading this myth prior to reading the play may make the discomfort Eliza feels and the detachment with which Henry views his "creation" more understandable. Note that unlike his counterpart in myth, Henry does not marry his creation; this difference is a good starting point for discussion of the play.

Another text ideally suited for pairing with *Pygmalion* is the popular musical *My Fair Lady*. This excellent adaptation of Shaw's story is readily available in both print and video form. A discussion of the changes made between the two texts could lead into a unit on rewriting or revising to suit an audience or to examination of other works that build on an earlier text, such as Tom Stoppard's *Rosencrantz and Guildenstern Are Dead* or Sir Walter Raleigh's "The Nymph's Reply to the Shepherd," written in response to Marlowe's poem "The Passionate Shepherd to His Love." Teachers could do similar comparisons by using texts and the films based on them and asking students to evaluate the changes made and theorize regarding purpose and suitability.

Teachers might also want to consider a unit of texts that draw on mythology as source material. Such a unit might include Mary Wollstonecraft Shelley's classic *Frankenstein,* subtitled *The Modern Prometheus;* James Joyce's *Ulysses* (a difficult text, but excerpted chapters are well within the reach of juniors and seniors); or Tennessee Williams's edgy Southern drama, *Orpheus Descending.*

More advanced classes might consider linking Henry Higgins's treatment of Eliza as an object to be toyed with to Tom Sawyer's demand that Jim play the role of proper prisoner before liberating him in Twain's *The Adventures of Huckleberry Finn* or to Torvald's treatment of Nora as a "pretty bird" in Ibsen's *A Doll's House.* Similarly, the idea of one person creating the image he or she seeks at any cost can be found in Browning's disturbing poem, "My Last Duchess." At the very least, teachers should point out that Shaw makes it clear that there will be no happy ending between Henry and Eliza and that there can be no happy ending when one person ignores another's humanity, no matter how noble their intentions.

Red Flags

None for American audiences, although the play contains a few words the British consider particularly offensive.

Suggested Grade

Suitable for all high school students. The play is probably too didactic in this form for ninth- or tenth-graders, however; teachers who want to use it for its connection to the Pygmalion myth should probably take an excerpt of the play or use *My Fair Lady* instead.

Film Versions

Pygmalion. Dir. Anthony Asquith and Leslie Howard. With Leslie Howard and Wendy Hiller. 1938. 95 min, B&W.

My Fair Lady (Musical version of *Pygmalion*). Dir. George Cukor. With Rex Harrison and Audrey Hepburn. 1964. 170 min. (G)

Critical Readings

Bloom, Harold, ed. *George Bernard Shaw's* Pygmalion. New York: Chelsea House, 1988. Nine essays on Shaw's themes, revision pattern, and focuses in *Pygmalion,* including a particularly interesting one by Lisë Pedersen on the comparison between *Pygmalion* and *Taming of the Shrew.*

A Raisin in the Sun   *1959*

Lorraine Hansberry

Characters: 8 Male; 3 Female
Leads: 6
Setting: The living room of a Southside Chicago apartment,
    late 1940s–early 1950s
Length: Full play

Synopsis

In *Raisin in the Sun,* a black family living together in a small apartment in Chicago
has hope appear, disappear, and then reappear once again. Lena Younger, the matri-
arch of the family, is due to come into $10,000 as a life insurance settlement. Her
son, Walter, living in the apartment with his wife, Ruth, and their ten-year-old son,
Travis, hopes to talk her into using the money as a down payment on a business,
but Lena is convinced that the best use for the money is to put part aside for her
daughter Beneatha to go to medical school and the rest into a house for the family
in a nice suburb. Walter is angered by her decision and feels strangled by the dead-
end job he holds and his lack of opportunities for advancement. His dreams are
dying. Ruth, it is revealed, is pregnant with a second child, something they cannot
afford. Ruth is desperate for the house and supports Lena, which further angers
Walter. Meanwhile, a spokesman for the neighborhood to which the Youngers plan
to move arrives and offers to buy the house back for more than they paid for it
rather than have a black family in the neighborhood. The Youngers angrily send
him away.

Thinking that she has to support her son's dreams, Lena tells Walter to take the
$6,500 not already paid into the new house and put $3,000 away for Beneatha. The rest,
she says, is for him to care for, to show he is the man of the family. Walter is elated and
rushes out shouting about the grand future he and his family have now. Unfortunately,
we learn that Walter gives all $6,500 to his friend Willy, one of his "partners" in the
business, and that Willy skips town with the cash. His dreams once again crushed, and
now responsible for destroying his sister's future, Walter appears completely broken.
Lena berates him for his selfishness. In a last-ditch effort to save something, Walter calls
the man from the neighborhood association and asks him to come by again, planning
to give in and sell back the house at a profit, despite the family's objections that giving
in to that sort of racism will leave them with nothing at all. In the final, climactic scene,
however, Walter looks at his son and refuses to sell out, realizing that the pride of a
working-class man who can finally afford a house is just as great as that of an executive
with a manor and a yacht. The family leaves for the new house with renewed hope and
strength.

Key Content Areas

Raisin is a play about the struggle of the working class, but it is equally a play about the struggle of black families. It would be a mistake to try to separate the two issues here because Hansberry has intertwined them carefully to produce a maximum effect. When Walter breaks down, it isn't just that he has a dead-end job that hurts him but that the job is so reminiscent of slavery. Beneatha's suitors, a black businessman who laughs at identity politics and an African scholar who encourages her to embrace her heritage, represent the two forces pulling on African Americans, each demanding complete obedience to their cause, and neither offering a compromise that best suits life in America for the average African American. The play tries to strike that balance to a certain extent; everything is clearly just a little harder, a little further out of reach for the black working class, but the *struggle* that the Youngers undergo resonates strongly with a broad range of American audiences.

Potential Connections/Ideas

The title of the play refers to Langston Hughes's famous poem "Harlem (a Dream Deferred)," which students should certainly read in conjunction with the play. Other texts which might prove valuable as connected works include August Wilson's play *Fences*, which is another story of a black working-class family struggling to make its way. The theme of a strong parent having to learn to listen to children is played out in Shakespeare's *The Tempest* and *King Lear*, as well as Gloria Naylor's novel *Mama Day*. The "sudden windfall" device as a way of triggering revelations about self and family is also used in Lillian Hellman's play *Toys in the Attic*, with powerful results. *Raisin* could even be paired with *Oedipus Rex* or a similar story of personal development and discovery by comparing Walter's growing understanding to that of the protagonist.

Red Flags

Two references to pregnancy, but little more.

Suggested Grade

A solid choice for all high school students. The action is straightforward enough that students of all ages should be able to look past it to examine the dynamics of the play and the issues it raises with minimal guidance from the teacher.

Film Versions

A Raisin in the Sun. Dir. Bill Duke. With Danny Glover and Esther Rolle. 1989. Made for TV. 171 min. (NR)

A Raisin in the Sun. Dir. Daniel Petrie. With Sidney Poitier and Ruby Dee. 1961. B&W, 128 min. (NR)

Critical Readings

Cheney, Anne. *Lorraine Hansberry.* Boston: Twayne, 1984. This book in the Twayne's United States Authors series provides full biographical information on Hansberry and a chapter devoted to *A Raisin in the Sun.* The chapter focuses particularly on the role Africa plays in the lives of African Americans and the place of women within African American culture and family life. It emphasizes the "universality" in Hansberry's message as partly responsible for the play's success with a wide range of audiences.

Washington, J. Charles. "*A Raisin in the Sun* Revisited." *Black American Literature Forum* 22.1 (Spring 1988): 109–24. A discussion of Walter, Lena, and their character development as logical and valuable within the context of African American history. The essay argues that Hansberry's play has lasting value as a source of universal hope as well as a barometer of the African American experience.

Wilkerson, Margaret B. "*A Raisin in the Sun:* Anniversary of an American Classic." *Theatre Journal* 38.4 (December 1986): 441–52. An essay that celebrates the twenty-fifth anniversary of *Raisin*'s Broadway opening. It discusses Hansberry's themes and the play's script alterations and restorations since the first staging, and it mentions an alternative, less "happy" ending that Hansberry wrote but later rejected.

Rosencrantz and Guildenstern Are Dead

1967

Tom Stoppard

Characters: 7–9 Male; 2–4 Female
Leads: 3
Setting: Places of no clear identity; various scenes in *Hamlet*
Length: Three acts

Synopsis

Rosencrantz and Guildenstern have been summoned to Claudius's court by special messenger. They travel there, but at the same time are slowly growing aware that something in their world is *not right*—randomness seems to have disappeared. On the way, they encounter traveling players who further confuse them. At length, they meet with Hamlet and attempt to understand why he has changed, but can find no answers. Unable to find a reason for anything that is happening, or even for their own participation, they decide to simply follow along and hope that things will work out. They accept Claudio's assignment, agreeing to accompany Hamlet to England and deliver a letter to the king. On the way, they discover the players on board with them and slowly realize that they, like the actors, can exist only in accordance with some sort of script. As the lights fade, so do Rosencrantz and Guildenstern, leaving only the conclusion of *Hamlet* behind.

Key Content Areas

Much like *Waiting for Godot*, this play is philosophical at heart. Why are we here? Where are we going? Has it been scripted for us? Are we bit players on a grand stage like Rosencrantz and Guildenstern? Also worth attention is the stylistic choice Stoppard makes in writing a play based on two marginal characters in another author's work.

Potential Connections/Ideas

The obvious approach to take with *Rosencrantz and Guildenstern Are Dead* is to assign the text in tandem with *Hamlet*. The two texts can be compared along several dimensions: Hamlet's point of view and Rosencrantz and Guildenstern's on life, fate, and destiny; the roles of the primary and secondary characters reversing from play to play; and the "real" world of *Hamlet* which contains the player's play, while in *Rosencrantz and*

Guildenstern Are Dead the players' play seems to contain the highly artificial world that the characters exist in. One might also ask if Rosencrantz and Guildenstern represent our modern feelings and Hamlet those of the sixteenth century.

Another option might be to explore "behind the scenes" of other plays and novels, looking at others that have been "altered" in rewrites or reimaginings, such as *Goodnight Desdemona (Good Morning Juliet)* by Ann-Marie MacDonald or John Gardner's *Grendel.* You might ask students to think about what goes on "offstage" in a book, movie, or play, and ask them to write their own version of such happenings in a favorite story. Pirandello's *Six Characters in Search of an Author* takes this concept a step further, showing us the desperate need of the actor for a script and leaving us wondering if we aren't equally desperate in our own lives.

Finally, *Rosencrantz and Guildenstern Are Dead* could easily be linked to *Waiting for Godot* as a pair of plays exploring Shakespeare's "all the world's a stage" metaphor. Such a discussion might be philosophically oriented, asking students to consider how they "act" in their day-to-day exchanges with others. Excerpts from Erving Goffman's classic analysis of human interaction, *The Presentation of Self in Everyday Life,* would provide extra fuel for this discussion.

Red Flags

A few double entendres and sexual references from the head player, but nothing too racy.

Suggested Grade

For teachers looking for a text to discuss in tandem with *Hamlet* or "backstage" discussions, this play will work with ninth-graders and up. Teachers who expect to discuss the philosophy behind the play as well as the plot, however, should limit its use to mature eleventh- or twelfth-grade classes.

Film Versions

Rosencrantz and Guildenstern Are Dead. Dir. Tom Stoppard. With Tim Roth, Gary Oldman, and Richard Dreyfuss. 1991. 118 min. (PG)

Critical Readings

Jenkins, Anthony. *Critical Essays on Tom Stoppard.* Boston: G. K. Hall and Co., 1990. Short, readable essays and essay excerpts on theme and philosophy in *Rosencrantz and Guildenstern Are Dead.*

School for Scandal

1777

Richard Sheridan

Characters: 11 Male; 4 Female
Leads: 5–6
Setting: Fashionable London, 1777
Length: Five acts

Synopsis

Lady Sneerwell, a notorious scandal-spreader, and her associate Snake have set out to meddle in the lives of Joseph and Charles Sample, brothers under the care of Sir Peter Teazle. Eager to secure Charles's hand for herself, Sneerwell agrees to help Joseph steal away Maria, Charles's beloved. Joseph, who has maintained a virtuous reputation despite his base morals, gladly plots with Sneerwell to deceive the community into denouncing Charles by spreading rumors of his dissolute behavior and wasteful ways in hopes that he will be able to claim his brother's share of their future inheritance from their Uncle Oliver, a businessman who has been abroad for many years.

Meanwhile, young Lady Teazle torments her much older husband with her extravagance and rudeness, mocking him for believing that he could marry a young woman at his age and hope for her to love him faithfully. She spends her time gossiping with Lady Sneerwell, much to Sir Peter's disgust, and begins an intrigue with Joseph as well, seduced by his promises of love. Joseph is not particularly interested in Lady Teazle but toys with her anyway as she foolishly risks her reputation.

Plagued by debts, Charles decides to sell his family portraits. An unabashed gamester and carouser, Charles is also good-natured and basically decent; his biggest fault is lack of self-control. Uncle Oliver returns home, however, and decides to check on his nephews. When he learns that Charles is selling the family portraits, he pretends to be a buyer to verify how low his nephew has sunk. Charles, however, surprises Oliver when he refuses to sell the portrait of Oliver, despite the disguised uncle's generous offers, and earns his affections by praising the supposedly absent relative.

A series of discoveries, culminating in the revelation of Lady Teazle hidden behind a screen in Joseph's apartment when her clandestine visit to flirt is interrupted, reveal Joseph's baseness and Charles's merit. Lady Teazle is embarrassed, but forgiven, and renounces her ill company; Joseph loses his potential inheritance, and Lady Sneerwell is left humiliated and the butt of scandal once more.

Key Content Areas

School for Scandal is a typical late-eighteenth-century comedy. It contains critiques of rakes, dissolute behavior, excess, and scandal-mongering ostensibly meant to reform the foolish. Also important to the play is Sheridan's critique of actual honor versus "reputation" and the relative importance of each, as well as the pleasure Londoners were taking in reading about scandals and intrigues.

Potential Connections/Ideas

One way to bring *School for Scandal* into the classroom is to consider the eighteenth-century shift from the straight comedy or farce to plays containing morality and didactic soliloquies. Sheridan's play and either Centlivre's *A Bold Stroke for a Wife* or *The Busybody* could easily be compared in this manner. From a historical point of view, the teacher could consider the development of the comedy as a genre, drawing on seventeenth- and nineteenth-century examples to complement Sheridan's work. This play can also be a starting point for an exploration of the London social world; such an exploration could include studies of some of the scandalous publications Sheridan rails against, such as Ned Ward's *The London Spy* or Delarivier Manley's masterpiece of mudslinging, *The New Atlantis*.

One might also link this play to the earlier, simpler "morality plays" that were regularly performed in pageants in centuries previous. Exploring similarities and differences might lead to some interesting discussions. Is Sheridan's moralizing genuinely meant, or is it added to mask the clever language and titillating intrigues of his play? What changes came with the onset of the Victorian period?

Red Flags

None. The "scandal" in this play is all talk.

Suggested Grade

Readable, witty, and fun; good for grades eight and up.

Film Versions

School for Scandal. Dir. Maurice Elvey. 1930. B&W, 75 min.

School for Scandal. Dir. Stuart Burge. 1975. UK television production.

Critical Readings

Auburn, Mark S. *Sheridan's Comedies: Their Contexts and Achievements*. Lincoln: University of Nebraska Press, 1977. 105-148. A thorough and very accessible discussion of

Sheridan's *School for Scandal* and its style, plus the elements that create positive audience response in each character. Highly recommended.

Durant, Jack D. *Richard Brinsley Sheridan*. Boston: Twayne, 1975. This book contains extensive background material on Sheridan, along with a chapter on *School for Scandal* (95–105) that is nowhere near as thorough as Auburn's work but still a useful summary of the play's action and themes.

She Stoops to Conquer   *1773*

Oliver Goldsmith

Characters: 6 Male; 4 Female
Leads: 5
Setting: A chamber in an old-fashioned house, an alehouse room, and outside; 1773
Length: Five acts

Synopsis

Mr. Hardcastle has invited Marlow, a worthy young gentleman, to his house in the country as a proposed match for his daughter Kate. Marlow's disposition, however, is well known. He is suitably rakish with "low women," but he cannot even speak to honorable women without blushing and stammering. Kate finds him a suitable match and decides to overcome his shyness by "stooping to conquer." She takes the guise of a chambermaid, to whom Marlow has no difficulty conveying his sentiments. Meanwhile, Tony Lumpkin, the spoiled son of Hardcastle's wife by a previous marriage, plots to deceive his mother and thus free himself from her desired match with his cousin Miss Neville. Hastings, Marlow's friend and Miss Neville's lover, plots to spirit her away, but the deceived Marlow accidentally spoils the plot. Finally, Marlow's father appears and reconciles Hardcastle to Marlow, who is himself undeceived by Kate. Mortified by his conduct, Marlow begs forgiveness from Hardcastle, who grants marriages all around as the play ends happily.

Key Content Areas

Arranged marriages and the difficulties they posed for women in the early eighteenth century. Also interesting is the gulf between the standards of conduct for polite society and for dealing with commoners that is so clearly illustrated by Marlow's dual behavior.

Potential Connections/Ideas

She Stoops to Conquer hinges on Marlow's strange unease with formal conversation with honorable women. Through the play, however, issues of propriety and manners are played upon—mothers who spoil their sons and let them become rakes, men who treat their host like an innkeeper and wonder at his conduct when he tries to treat them as fellow gentlemen, and women who at turns play impudent and piously obedient in order to work around the rules men set for them. Aside from the feminist questions that would certainly be worth exploring in *She Stoops to Conquer*, explorations could be continued within the eighteenth century with Eliza Haywood's play *Fantomina* or her novel *Love in Excess,* or could be tied to Shakespeare's *Twelfth Night* or Kate Chopin's *The Awakening.* It might prove interesting for students to spend a unit on the culture of manners that existed in England in the eighteenth and nineteenth centuries. Students could trace the English tradition of self-examination and critique from this play to Sheridan's *School for Scandal;* to the novels of Jane Austen and the nineteenth-century classic novel on the subject, Thackeray's *Vanity Fair;* and perhaps even to an operetta such as *Patience* or *The Mikado,* two of Gilbert and Sullivan's popular works ridiculing the English crazes for the aesthetic movement and all things Japanese in the late nineteenth and early twentieth centuries.

Red Flags

A few suggestive puns, but nothing risqué.

Suggested Grade

A lighthearted comedy of errors suitable for all high school students.

Critical Readings

Brooks, Christopher K. "Goldsmith's Feminist Drama: *She Stoops to Conquer,* Silence, and Language." *Papers on Language and Literature* 28 (Winter 1992): 38–51. A heavily academic paper arguing that *She Stoops to Conquer* is an early feminist text and that Kate Hardcastle is an example of the emerging power of women in the eighteenth century.

The Still Alarm

1925

George S. Kaufman

Characters: 5 Male; 0 Female
Leads: 4
Setting: A suite in a hotel
Length: One act

Synopsis

The Still Alarm is a short play with a simple plot: Two gentlemen are informed that their hotel is on fire, and two firemen come to fight the blaze. What makes the play remarkable is the very casual way the scene unfolds and the absolute lack of disturbance the actors are instructed to show in reading their lines. As the curtain rises, Ed and Bob, two businessmen, are saying goodbye at Bob's hotel room door. Bob remembers that he wants to show Ed the plans for his new house and invites his friend back in. The two are just looking over the plans when the bellboy arrives with a message for Bob: The hotel is on fire. Ed inquires if the fire is particularly bad and, when assured that the hotel looks as if it will burn down (they verify this for themselves at the window), declares that they probably ought to leave.

The two *don't* leave, however. They continue to casually discuss the fire's progress, noting that it has consumed all the floors below their own, but that the upper floors are still intact. Bob reminds the bellboy that he really ought to notify the fire department, and Ed tells the boy to let the chief (an old school friend) know that Ed Jamison asked him to call. The bellboy is tipped and dismissed, and the men turn again to a discussion of how they really ought to leave soon. Bob begins packing but is distracted by Ed's admiration of his house plans. He briefly flirts with the idea of seeking another room at a different hotel but drops the idea because other hotels might be on fire as well. At least he knows about this one.

Ed, getting a bit warm, orders up some ice water. The firemen arrive soon after, shown in by the bellboy. One is carrying a hose, the other a violin case. After introductions, the firemen explain that they ought to get to work, and Ed and Bob step aside. Sid, the second fireman, begins tuning his violin at once, as the first fireman explains that this is really the only opportunity he gets to practice, in that much of their work is waiting around for walls to collapse. He then turns his attention to the fire, determining at once that the room next door would be a much better spot to fight from. He calls down and requests that the key be sent up at once. Meanwhile, Bob offers the fireman a chair, and Ed provides him with a cigar, which he lights out the window off the flames rising from the floor below. Sid indicates he is ready to play, and the curtain falls on the three men listening attentively to the fine recital and occasionally mopping their brows.

106

Key Content Areas

The Still Alarm sits somewhere on the line between burlesque and farce. The characters are caricatures, present only enough to create the ludicrousness of the situation, but at the same time Kaufman's insistence that the characters must never raise their voices or act as if anything but a polite gathering is underway is clearly poking fun at the stereotype of the unflappable Englishman. In either case, the plot is there for service alone; the comic value of the play comes not from action but rather from the characters' reactions (or absurd lack thereof) to the fire.

Potential Connections/Ideas

The Still Alarm is an excellent example of farce, and its short length makes it ideal for use as a filler between larger works. It could easily be worked into a unit on the variations of the comedy, a unit that might also include examples of Renaissance comedies (Shakespeare's *Much Ado about Nothing*, Ben Jonson's *Volpone*), Restoration comedies, comedies of manners (Wycherley's *The Country Wife*, Etherege's *The Man of Mode*), absurdism (Ionesco's *The Bald Soprano*, Beckett's *Waiting for Godot*), and modern comedies such as Neil Simon's *Plaza Suite* or Noël Coward's *Blithe Spirit.*

As a highly stylized work that depends largely on the staging and situation instead of characters, *The Still Alarm* can demonstrate the range of artifice in the modern theater. Other plays that could be used in such a presentation include Samuel Beckett's *Happy Days,* in which the leading character is buried in an ever-increasing pile of dirt; David Ives's *Sure Thing,* in which two would-be lovers are allowed to go back and try again each time they say the wrong thing during a first meeting; Anna Deavere Smith's *Fires in the Mirror,* in which one actor portrays more than thirty characters through a series of connected monologues; and Byron's *Manfred,* a text written in dramatic form but never intended for performance. Teachers might use these works as an entry to a unit on creative expression and experimentation, urging students to modify traditional art forms or create new ones to spark audience reaction or to startle readers out of the comfort of their expectations.

Red Flags

None.

Suggested Grade

Most high school students should find the plot device—characters so cultured they don't react to *anything* with alarm—obvious enough, but younger students and less advanced readers may need to hear the text read out loud to completely understand how the comedy materializes without jokes.

Film Versions

The Still Alarm. With Fred Allen and Clifton Webb. 1930. Short film.

Critical Readings

This one-act comedy sketch has little material for critics to draw on for analysis, but the two books below provide good background material on Kaufman and his more prominent works, as well as short mention of *The Still Alarm.*

Goldstein, Malcolm. *George S. Kaufman: His Life, His Theater.* New York: Oxford University, 1979.

Pollack, Rhoda-Gale. *George S. Kaufman.* Boston: Twayne, 1988.

Sure Thing

1988

David Ives

Characters: 1 Male; 1 Female
Leads: 2 (plus bell ringer)
Setting: A café table, present day
Length: One act

Synopsis

Sure Thing opens with the arrival of Bill, a man in his early twenties, who walks up to Betty, a woman in her twenties who is reading *The Sound and the Fury* at a small table in a restaurant. He asks her if he might sit down, and she refuses—and a bell rings. The two move back to their starting places, and Bill tries his approach again. This time, he gets a bit further with Betty, but quickly enough he missteps, the bell rings again, and the two start again from a few lines earlier. Ives uses this technique to lead us through all the possible miscues that can destroy "love at first sight," from politics to personal problems to ex-girlfriends and lesbian lovers. After about fifteen minutes of blundering, Bill and Betty finally find the right lines and leave to spend the rest of their lives together.

Key Content Areas

Ives is playing with two ideas here: the much desired ideal of "love at first sight" and the notion of basing a play on all the possible outcomes of a single question. Secondary to this would be issues regarding gender stereotyping, which is used extensively for comic purposes. (It can be entertaining to swap readers, with a male reading Betty and a female reading Bill, as a way of exploring the stereotyping issue.)

Potential Connections/Ideas

As a play of repetitions and possibilities, *Sure Thing* would fit well as a lead-in to the more complex Beckett play *Waiting for Godot* and a discussion of modernist plays or of the idea of "play" within a work. One could also use this play as a bridge to or from a discussion of our notions of romance as genre and of "romance" in general, perhaps as a lead-in to one of Shakespeare's romantic comedies of mistaken identities, such as *Twelfth Night,* or an eighteenth-century comedy such as Centlivre's *A Bold Stroke for a Wife.* If you're interested in discussing gender stereotyping and its purposes, you might move to Eliza Haywood's short play *Fantomina.* Caryl Churchill's *Cloud 9* is one of the most famous plays that question the traditional gender roles; if you prefer novels, try Charlotte Perkins Gilman's *Herland*. For a younger audience or one more interested in fantasy or science fiction, you could recommend any of Anne McCaffrey's *Pern* novels as a way to continue gender boundary discussions. Finally, for more works that question the order of things or play with the boundaries of their genre ("experimental" works), Don DeLillo's *White Noise,* Tim O'Brien's war novel *Going after Cacciato,* and Ann-Marie MacDonald's clever play *Goodnight Desdemona (Good Morning Juliet)* are all excellent choices.

Red Flags

Sure Thing has very little objectionable material within it: one appearance of a major obscenity, one short harangue on male behavior after sex, one or two jokes with hints of homosexuality, and, if you really stretch it, one possible incest joke.

Suggested Grade

This play would be acceptable for grades eight and up, though some jokes might go over the heads of students below tenth or eleventh grade.

Tartuffe

1664

Jean-Baptiste Molière

Characters: 7 Male; 5 Female
Leads: 4–5
Setting: Orgon's bourgeois home in Paris
Length: Five acts

Synopsis

Orgon, a wealthy landowner, has fallen under the influence of a "pious man" named Tartuffe. Penniless before Orgon becomes his patron, Tartuffe now holds a position of power in the household, causing the friends of Orgon's children to be turned away and producing a falling out between Orgon and his son. Even Mariane, Orgon's obedient daughter, is compelled to turn against Orgon when he tries to force her to marry Tartuffe instead of Valère, to whom she was earlier promised. Cléante, Orgon's brother-in-law, warns him he is making a grave mistake in trusting Tartuffe, but Orgon, incensed at his family's disobedience, signs a writ willing his house to Tartuffe. Finally, Orgon's family sets up Tartuffe, revealing to Orgon that his religious adviser has been trying to seduce his wife, Elmire. Orgon angrily orders Tartuffe to leave, but Tartuffe quickly sends a process server to evict the family, then follows with an accusation of treason against Orgon supported by papers Orgon had given him for safekeeping. Valère tries to spirit Orgon away, but Tartuffe leads the police to them before they can escape. All seems lost until the policeman reveals that he is there to arrest Tartuffe, who is a well-known con artist, and whom the king had been watching as he took advantage of Orgon. In gratitude, Orgon promises Mariane to Valère once again, and the family sets off for the palace to give thanks to the king.

Key Content Areas

Tartuffe is primarily a social satire, playing on the dangers of both excessive faith and excessive credulity. Its tongue-lashing, however, is not for religion itself, but for those who seek to abuse religion by perverting it to their own needs. It is also clearly a fore-runner to many of the Restoration comedies in England, which center on a young couple trying to get married despite the opposition of a foolish father or guardian.

Potential Connections/Ideas

As a play considered *too* direct in its critique of the church in its time, *Tartuffe* is ideal for use with the *Canterbury Tales* as a way of highlighting the use of popular forms and stories to protest a powerful social institution, the church. Both authors take care to include generous amounts of pro-religious material as padding for their cutting attacks on corrupt religious figures and "overpious" swindlers. *Tartuffe* would also make a good entry to Restoration comedy in English literature and could be compared with Wycherley's *The Country Wife* or Goldsmith's *She Stoops to Conquer* in its use of the disguised lover as comic trick. *Tartuffe* could also be worked into a discussion of the world of oratory and politics, examining those who use hyperbole as a means of persuasion and the effectiveness of the technique on the unwary.

Red Flags

None. *Tartuffe* is free of profanity. Although Tartuffe's exposure scene contains a great deal of hinting about Tartuffe's sexual demands and Elmire's anxious wondering as to when Orgon will intervene, the innuendo is mild, and harder to follow than what you'd find in a PG movie.

Suggested Grade

This play is suitable for grades eight and up; even young readers should be able to appreciate its message of "moderation in all things."

Film Versions

Tartuffe. Dir. Basil Coleman. With Michael Craig and Michael Holdern. 1971. UK TV production.

Tartuffe. Dir. Bill Alexander. With Antony Sher and Nigel Hawthorne. 1984. 110 min. A Royal Shakespeare Company production. (NR)

Le Tartuffe. Dir. Gerard Depardieu. With Gerard Depardieu. 1984. (English subtitles.)

Critical Readings

Gossman, Lionel. *Men and Masks: A Study of Molière*. Baltimore: Johns Hopkins University P, 1963. Contains a heavily academic analysis of *Le Tartuffe* that is enlightening but assumes both a working knowledge of French (quotes from the play are not translated) and an understanding of concepts such as nominalism and the possessive/reconstructive patriarchal gaze.

Guicharnaud, Jacques, ed. *Molière: A Collection of Critical Essays*. Englewood Cliffs, NJ: Prentice Hall, 1964. A very broad look at elements of Molière's style, such as voice, speech, farce, and the comic vision, spread over a number of excerpts and short essays. Useful, but specific information can be difficult to locate.

Howarth, W. D. *Molière: A Playwright and His Audience.* New York: Cambridge University P, 1982. A good overview of social, political, and religious conditions in Molière's day, plus short commentary on *Tartuffe* as a play about Orgon and his foolish blindness to the reality of Tartuffe rather than about Tartuffe's own duplicity.

The Teahouse of the August Moon   1952

John Patrick

Characters: 13+ Male; 8+ Female
Leads: 6
Setting: Occupied Japan, the years following the end of World War II
Length: Full play

Synopsis

The opening scene of *Teahouse* sets the stage for what is to come. We meet Sakini, a middle-aged Okinawan who clearly views the entire scene with great amusement and approaches his narration as if he was bringing us in on a joke that those involved somehow miss. Sakini introduces us to his commander, Colonel Purdy, and at the same time to the childlike manner he takes on to befuddle the occupying army. It is clear he is far cleverer than the colonel and by implication, everyone else in the army.

The colonel decides to ship Sakini off to the small village of Tobiki with Captain Fisby, a new arrival who has been transferred through nearly every division in the Army. Purdy thinks he's getting rid of two of his problems by ordering them to implement "Plan B" in the village: constructing a schoolhouse and building a practicing democracy. Fisby begins with the best of intentions, making a speech to the people of Tobiki and encouraging them to appoint their own police and agriculture chiefs.

Where Fisby encounters trouble, however, is in the gifts he is given by the villagers. They include a geisha named Lotus Blossom, a lovely woman who begins causing difficulties in the village as she attracts the attention of the men and the jealousy of the women. Sakini explains that the women want what she has—doesn't democracy mean that everyone is equal?—so Fisby finds himself asking Lotus Blossom to open a school and teach the women her craft. Meanwhile, the men of the village are dissatisfied as well. They have taken a vote, and they do not want a school—they want a teahouse. A teahouse, they explain, would be a source of pride and a place where they could spend the money that Fisby hopes they will make by selling local crafts. Again, Sakini points out that democracy is supposed to rule, and Fisby begins construction of the teahouse.

Purdy, who hasn't received a report from Fisby in a month, sends a psychiatrist to Tobiki to see what has happened, but Fisby converts him to his own "rebuilding" effort. Unfortunately, sales of crafts go very poorly, and the villagers are about to give up and get drunk when Fisby discovers that they make a fabulous brandy from sweet potatoes. Suddenly the village is wealthy and happy, with hundreds of stills producing all that the occupation forces can drink. Purdy discovers this, however, and comes to set things right. He orders the stills destroyed and the teahouse torn down; the villagers reluctantly comply. Fisby is to be court-martialed, and he has just said his good-byes to the village when Purdy comes in, distraught. He has received word that his report was misread in Washington, and that the government is so proud of Tobiki's success that it wants to make it a feature story. Sakini interrupts the colonel's moaning to tell him that the stills are really still there and that the teahouse can be put back together in minutes—the destruction was faked just to satisfy those strange Americans. The play closes with everyone happy and Sakini reminding us just who is really running the show.

Key Content Areas

The occupation of Japan and the rationalization of forcibly bringing "democracy" to a people who view you as yet another in a series of invaders provide the main content of the play. Although the issue is treated with a comic tone, there is an inescapable note of seriousness to it, visible each time a villager bows submissively or Sakini calls someone "boss."

Potential Connections/Ideas

Teahouse of the August Moon is a farce of sorts that reminds you in turn of *South Pacific, Madame Butterfly,* and the variety of "trickster" farces involving characters such as Scapin, Harlequin, or Trickster Monkey, depending on the culture in question.

The more serious issue of forced occupation of a country by a standing army is also addressed in a number of works. Along these lines, it resembles Brian Friel's magnificent play, *Translations.* It could also be taught in tandem with Jamaica Kincaid's angry condemnation of colonialism, *A Small Place,* or the classic tale of cultural misunderstanding and prejudice, *A Passage to India* by E. M. Forster. Finally, the British occupation of Africa is dramatized in Wole Soyinka's *Death and the King's Horseman,* with much darker results.

Red Flags

The geisha trade is mistaken for prostitution by Americans who don't understand it. Brandy sales save the village. One officer gets drunk.

Suggested Grade

Suitable for all grades. The story is witty and clever, and students will have no trouble following the action. As a result, they should find it easy to discuss the material in a more serious manner or to use it as a segue into darker views of colonialism.

Film Versions

Teahouse of the August Moon. Dir. Daniel Mann. With Marlon Brando. 1956. 123 min. (NR)

Toys in the Attic   *1959*

Lillian Hellman

Characters: 7 Male; 4 Female
Leads: 6
Setting: A poor neighborhood in New Orleans, 1959
Length: Full play

Synopsis

Toys in the Attic opens in the living room of the Bernier house, a well-kept but clearly old and rickety home on the bayou. Two sisters, Anna and Carrie, have been making do in this house for years, saving a portion of each paycheck for their dream trip to Europe— a trip we quickly learn the two have been talking of for years that is really just a symbol of the hope they share of escaping the frustrations of their unpleasant jobs and their lonely lives. The two are also worried about their brother, Julian, who always seems to be in need of money and who has disappeared from his last known address without contacting them.

Soon Mrs. Albertine Prine, a rich widow, enters the scene. She is an odd woman, looking on the Berniers with some distaste, but at the same time carrying on an affair with Henry, her African American chauffeur. She informs the sisters that Julian is in town and that he will be bringing to visit them his new wife—her daughter, Lily. Julian enters soon after, armed with a fleet of gifts and informing the sisters that everything is going to be different from now on. Come tomorrow, Julian says, he will be a rich man, and all the Berniers' dreams will come true.

Unfortunately, money doesn't bring happiness for the Bernier family. In fact, Julian's new wealth quickly destroys the family. Lily, his wife, seems to have the mind of a child; she is obsessed with having Julian to herself and is happier when the two are poor and alone than rich with his family. Anna and Carrie begin to feud as well. When Carrie threatens to interfere in Julian's marriage, Anna accuses her of choosing to remain single because she has always wanted Julian.

In Act 3, the dreams of the Berniers fall apart. Julian has successfully blackmailed a corrupt but powerful man and goes to split the take with his accomplice, the man's ex-wife. Lily, however, is so intent on returning to the way things were before that she calls the victim and tells him where to find Julian. Julian returns home beaten badly, his money lost. Carrie and Anna are aware of what Lily has done, but rather than destroy Julian's one remaining joy, they keep silent. Again they find themselves emptying their savings account to lend Julian money to start over one more time, and they return to their grinding jobs, starting over in what we now know will be a hopeless struggle to escape.

Key Content Areas

Toys in the Attic is an examination of family relations, specifically the roles of "the oldest" and "the youngest." It covers issues of class difference and touches on race relations as well. The sacrifices of the female characters and their various motives provide copious material for discussion.

Potential Connections/Ideas

This play could be taught as a companion to other stories of families in conflict, such as *King Lear* or August Wilson's *Fences*. The complex relationships among sisters is the focus of Jane Smiley's novel *A Thousand Acres*. The problems of marriage between classes are examined in novels such as *Mansfield Park* and *Jane Eyre*. Students might be able to relate to the struggle of the sisters to escape the day-to-day drudgery of their lives; modern stories of this sort include James Thurber's short story "The Secret Life of Walter Mitty" and Kate Chopin's *The Awakening*. A short lesson might also connect the sisters' lives to Langston Hughes's famous poem "Harlem (a Dream Deferred)."

Red Flags

Although largely inoffensive, *Toys in the Attic* does contain a scene in which Lily pulls Julian's hand to her breast and suggests they go to bed together. There is a moment where Anna accuses her sister of being in love with their brother, and an extramarital affair from the past is revealed as well. Teachers should also note that the glossed-over relationship between Henry and Mrs. Prine fuels some racist comments during the play that are presented in almost a throwaway manner and that should not be ignored; rather, they should be used as an opportunity to discuss the way biases embedded in a culture often surface in its literature as issues, even when they seem entirely unrelated to the literature's purpose.

Suggested Grade

Though not particularly graphic, especially by current standards, the sexual suggestion here, combined with Anna's implication that Carrie is in love with Julian, may be more than some teachers want to bring into the classroom. A mature ninth-grade class should be able to handle this work, properly supervised.

Film Versions

Toys in the Attic. Dir. George Roy Hill. With Dean Martin and Geraldine Page. 1963. B&W, 90 min. (NR)

Critical Readings

Lederer, Katherine. *Lillian Hellman.* Boston: Twayne, 1979. Another volume in the Twayne's United States Authors series, this text contains an overview of Hellman's tempestuous life and career, as well as a short discussion of *Toys in the Attic* as a dramatic fable, rather than tragicomedy or problem play.

The Tragical History of Doctor Faustus

1604

Christopher Marlowe

Characters: 19+ Male; 3+ Female
Leads: 2
Setting: Courts, universities, and similar locations around the world
Length: Thirteen scenes

Synopsis

Marlowe's version of the classic story of Faustus is arguably the best of the lot. The plot is fairly simple and straightforward; the play opens with a brief description of Faustus's birth and education. He has risen rapidly in stature in the academic community in Wittenberg to become the greatest of the scholars there, but he has also become bored with his studies. Casting off philosophy, law, medicine, and divinity in turn as too simple for his powerful mind, Faustus turns to necromancy, or black magic, as the ultimate intellectual pursuit.

Against the warnings of a good angel and some of his peers, Faustus delves into the dark arts, learning to raise spirits. He calls forth Mephistophilis, a powerful demon, and demands that the spirit serve him, but the demon refuses, saying that he owes obedience to Lucifer and none else. Eager for the power Mephistophilis can bring and certain that hell is nothing more than a myth the church uses to herd the masses, Faustus offers his eternal soul to Lucifer in exchange for twenty-four years of absolute service from Mephistophilis. Lucifer agrees, and Faustus signs his soul away with his own blood.

For the next twenty-four years, Faustus lives a life of luxury, indulging himself with travel and gathering all the knowledge he could possibly hope for. He learns how the world operates, masters the sciences, and even calls up figures from history, including Alexander the Great. To satisfy his lust, he takes Helen of Troy as a concubine. He plays pranks on the pope and visits the courts of emperors and kings. From time to time, he considers the danger of his bargain and is tempted to repent, but each time he decides that God would never listen to the prayers of a soul as black as his. Mephistophilis also intimidates Faustus when he comes too close to repentance, reminding him of their bargain and threatening him with torture. Faustus quickly turns back to Lucifer each time, abandoning his potential salvation.

Finally, the twenty-four years have come to an end, and it is Faustus's final night on earth. In his final hour, Faustus bemoans the choice he made and begs heaven for a chance to repent. All avenues seem closed to him, however; God rejects his pleas, and the sciences he put so much stock in fail him, leaving him trapped at the mercy of Lucifer. Cursing himself and the temptations of Lucifer, he is carried off by devils to his eternal torment as the curtain closes.

Key Content Areas

Doctor Faustus is an exemplum in drama form. It preaches that seeking to rise above the human station tempts divine wrath and punishment for pride. Faustus's fall is more the result of his pride than of any other vice; although he lusts and is greedy, the doctor above all believes himself too bright for earthly intellectual pursuits and seeks to become as powerful as a god through his studies and magic. Even so, the play also teaches that salvation is always within reach, unless we persuade ourselves to ignore it.

Potential Connections/Ideas

Doctor Faustus is based on the often told "bargain with the Devil" folktales and is one of the most popular variants of this type of story. Teachers who are including a unit on the transmission of folktales or on variant forms of stories through the ages may want to consider teaching this play together with Goethe's version, *Faust,* or with Lord Byron's poem-play *Manfred.* In "The Devil and Tom Walker," a short story by Washington Irving, the title character bargains with the Devil for riches and power, only to later regret his choice. Stephen Vincent Binét's "The Devil and Daniel Webster" is a similar tale, but the Devil is outfoxed by the famed politician.

Teachers may also wish to incorporate *Doctor Faustus* into units on the tragic hero, focusing on Faustus's hubris. In this context, works such as Shakespeare's *King Lear* and Theodore Dreiser's *Sister Carrie* offer additional opportunities for connection and discussion, along with classic examples of the tragic hero such as Oedipus or modern examples, such as Tom Wolfe's *The Bonfire of the Vanities* or Arthur Miller's *Death of a Salesman.* Alternatively, *Doctor Faustus* can be compared with earlier morality plays, such as *Everyman,* and with other versions of the exemplum, such as the chivalric tales of King Arthur's court, or William Hogarth's various series of engravings on morality, including "Industry and Idleness," "The Rake's Progress," and "The Harlot's Progress." Such works might provide interesting comparisons of the methods used to impress the need for morality on audiences over the course of literary history.

Red Flags

In two scenes, characters talk about the sexual favors they will obtain as a result of black magic. Neither is particularly graphic, but neither is subtle in the suggestion of lechery, either. Excising the two low comedy scenes, however, is a simple task and does not affect the focus of the text or the continuity of the action in the slightest.

Suggested Grade

The tale itself is not beyond the reach of younger students and is appropriate as an example of the tragic hero and the concept of hubris. The play is short, easier to understand than *Oedipus Rex,* and therefore a good choice for freshman or sophomore English classes, provided the sexually suggestive scenes (Scenes 4 and 6) are cut. Seniors will find the direct language of Shakespeare's contemporary in sharp contrast to the flowery style of the Bard's plays and will be better equipped to explore modern works for having studied one of the most influential stories in literature.

Film Versions

Doctor Faustus. Dir. Richard Burton and Nevill Coghill. With Richard Burton and Elizabeth Taylor. 1968. 93 min. (NR)

Critical Readings

Greg, W. W. "The Damnation of Faustus." *Marlowe: A Collection of Critical Essays.* Ed. Clifford Leech. Englewood Cliffs, NJ: Prentice Hall, 1964. 92–107. An essay tracking Faustus's moral disintegration from a man seeking knowledge at any cost to a hedonist.

Translations   *1980*

Brian Friel

Characters: 7 Male; 3 Female
Leads: 3–4
Setting: A hedge-school in an Irish-speaking community in County Donegal, 1833
Length: Three acts

Synopsis

Hugh and his lame son, Manus, teach Latin at a small school in Baile Beag, or Ballybeg, as the English call it. They and the community are surprised and pleased when Hugh's younger son, Owen, returns to the town with a surveying and cartography team of English soldiers, come to map the country. Owen, acting as translator for both the soldiers and the community people, brings the two sides together in a friendly manner. A young lieutenant named Yolland who is part of the survey crew is particularly smitten with the town and with the Irish language, and even more so with Maire, a young townswoman who wants to learn English. Caught between the cultured English world and his own history, however, Owen finds himself helping to break down Irish culture as often as preserving it. Yolland and Maire's budding romance offers hope that the two cultures can grow to understand one another, but when Yolland vanishes one night, the hope is dashed, as the army threatens to systematically destroy the parish until his return—a return we know will never occur.

Key Content Areas

Translations is rich in discussion topics, most centered around the overarching theme of colonialism. Issues of language and its use are also important, particularly in terms of the bind in which it puts Owen (who finds himself needing to sacrifice both his language and his identity to succeed in English society) and the romantic stumblings of Yolland and Maire. The hedge-school system and the literacy movement of the period might also be of some historical interest to readers.

Potential Connections/Ideas

Because *Translations* is an excellent example of Irish political theater, it is ideal for use as an interdisciplinary bridge between a European history class and an English class. Such a pairing could stand on its own but would be extremely effective as part of a long-term examination of the literature of colonialism. Studying works such as Wole Soyinka's

Death and the King's Horseman, Michelle Cliff's *No Telephone to Heaven,* or Chinua Achebe's famous novel *Things Fall Apart* would offer students a set of viewpoints from the colonized cultures, viewpoints not normally offered but just now beginning to find space for themselves within our literary world. Such discussions might branch out into questions regarding America's status as a colonizing nation, or whether minority cultures that have willingly immigrated to the United States ought to be considered in the same light as the Irish in English-occupied Ireland or the many European and American colonies in Africa. Of course, a teacher could also easily spend a unit on Irish theater and its development as political voice, in which case I recommend an anthology such as the W. W. Norton *Modern Irish Drama* as a good starting point.

Red Flags

Translations, like much of modern Irish drama, relies heavily on stereotypical characters. Some might be offended at first by stock characters such as the farm boy, the comely Irish lass hunting for a wealthy husband, or the drunken old man who plays the fool. It might be worthwhile to ask your class why an Irish author would use such unflattering stereotypes in his plays, and Friel, in fact, uses them regularly.

Suggested Grade

The text contains little a ninth-grader could not understand, but discussions of colonialism might be best left to tenth- and eleventh-graders who have studied enough European and American history to make useful links.

Critical Readings

Maxwell, D. E. S. *Brian Friel.* Cranbury, NJ: Associated University Presses, 1973. Although published too early to contain information on *Translations,* this short biography and critical overview discusses Friel's major influences and themes—particularly the conflict between the restrictive lifestyle of Ireland and the longing for return that many of its émigrés seem to feel, despite having left to escape those restrictions and often crushing poverty, and how this conflict is played out in the use of language and search for identity in Friel's plays.

Schrank, Bernice, and William W. Demastes. *Irish Playwrights, 1880–1995: A Research and Production Sourcebook.* Westport, CT: Greenwood P, 1997. 97–107. Contains only *very* sketchy information on Friel and his work but worth mentioning for its helpful bibliography of recent essays and books on Friel.

Trifles

1916

Susan Glaspell

Characters: 3 Male; 2 Female
Leads: 5
Setting: The kitchen of a country farmhouse, early 1900s
Length: One act

Synopsis

John Wright, a farmer, is dead, and his wife is in jail, suspected of his murder. Sheriff Peters; Henderson, the young county attorney; and Lewis Hale, Wright's neighbor, come to the Wright house to look for clues or evidence. Accompanying them are Mrs. Peters and Mrs. Hale, who have come to pick up clothing for Mrs. Wright and to check to see if her preserves are still intact or destroyed by the cold in the abandoned house.

The men enter first and immediately notice that the kitchen is in disarray. Pots are unwashed, the counter is dirty, and the towels have been used. Henderson remarks that Mrs. Wright wasn't a very good housekeeper, and Hale dismisses the request to check on the preserves as typical of women—always concerned with trifles. The three head upstairs to check the bedroom where the death took place, leaving the women behind.

Mrs. Hale and Mrs. Peters see the room in a very different way. They look at the disarray with sympathy for Mrs. Wright, wondering what it must be like to have strangers poking through your house and searching for things to turn against you. They resent the patronizing comments about "trifles" and the way that the men assume that things like an unmade bed or an unwashed pot are merely "bad house-keeping"—and as a result, they see far more in the kitchen then the men do.

As Mrs. Hale picks up the clothing for Mrs. Wright, she tells Mrs. Peters how the new widow had seemed to disappear from the town over the past years and how she used to be a beautiful, lively girl singing in the town choir. Mr. Wright, she says, was a good man but a loner, and very grim; he liked peace and quiet, and that, she supposes, kept Mrs. Wright at home and away from society. While chatting, Mrs. Hale looks over Mrs. Wright's quilting, wondering if they should take it to her in prison. On closer inspection, however, the two women notice how the stitching, neat and tight elsewhere, is badly out of line and confused on the last panel.

Mrs. Peters, looking for something to wrap the sewing in, comes across an empty birdcage in a closet. The two wonder what happened to the bird, figuring that it must have been Mrs. Wright's one solace out there alone. In packing up the sewing, they discover a small box wrapped in silk. Inside is the bird, its neck broken, twisted until it couldn't breathe.

Mrs. Peters and Mrs. Hale are able to put two and two together quickly enough, but they also realize that their lives have, at times, been much like Mrs. Wright's. As the men return downstairs, the two women exchange a quick glance, and when the men once again dismiss what they have been doing as women's trifles, they remain silent—just as the men expect.

Key Content Areas

Trifles is an early feminist work, one which derives its strength and substance from its portrayal of the ways men and women interact and the assumptions each makes about the other. Glaspell's piece neither praises nor denounces Mrs. Wright's actions; rather, it seeks to make us aware of the conditions that led to the murder by showing us the lack of awareness men have of the indicators in a woman's world and the ease with which they discard the tasks women of the period spend their lives on as "trifles."

Potential Connections/Ideas

Trifles is a short play, perhaps twelve pages long. Its brevity allows it to be paired easily with other texts, possibly as an in-class reading assignment leading up to an exploratory writing or comparison piece. Its look at the tensions faced by women make it a good partner piece for many nineteenth-century novels and stories, including Kate Chopin's *The Awakening*, Willa Cather's *A Lost Lady*, or Charlotte Perkins Gilman's *The Yellow Wallpaper*. Ibsen's *A Doll's House* also explores the tensions between a man who dominates his household and his wife, who finally is forced to act to relieve the stifling pressure she is feeling.

Although it is easy to explore Glaspell's work as a feminist text, it is also an excellent example of a mystery that can be used as part of a unit on the mystery as literary form. Comparable works that produce their tension through psychological pressure rather than direct action include Poe's classic story *The Tell-Tale Heart*, Jacobs and Parker's short play *The Monkey's Paw*, and Agatha Christie's novel *Ten Little Indians*.

Red Flags

None.

Suggested Grade

Suitable for all high school students. For freshmen and sophomores, the play may be best used as an introduction to the concept of point of view and its importance as a device for plot and character development. For juniors and seniors, the significance of the play as an early feminist text and as part of an emerging new voice in literature can be emphasized.

Film Versions

A Jury of Her Peers. Dir. Sally Heckel. 1980. Short film.

Critical Readings

Ben-Zvi, Linda. "'Murder, She Wrote': The Genesis of Susan Glaspell's *Trifles*." *Theater Journal* 44.2 (May 1992): 141–62. A thorough discussion of the source story for *Trifles* and the thematic importance of Glaspell's adaptation of the actual events the play is based on.

The Visit

1956

Friedrich Dürrenmatt

Characters: Up to 20 Male; up to 20 Female
Leads: 2
Setting: Guellen, a small town "somewhere in Central Europe," 1956
Length: Full play

Synopsis

The action of *The Visit* opens on a town clearly dying. Nearly all businesses have closed, the town hall is to be repossessed, and the Guellen History Museum has been "sold to America" to try to keep the town alive. There is a great stir, however, over the pending visit of the elderly millionaire Claire Zachanassian, who grew up in Guellen but left years ago in shame, pregnant with the child of Alfred Ill, "the most popular man" in town. Now her return and her philanthropic history promise hope for the town, but her arrival attaches an unexpected condition to Guellen's recovery. Zachanassian offers to give the town a million dollars—but only if someone agrees to give her the justice she seeks. Years ago, Ill bribed two witnesses to lie in a paternity trial to rid himself of Claire and her child; Claire has had each of them blinded and castrated as revenge. Now she demands that Ill be killed if Guellen wants her money.

Although the townspeople at first refuse the offer in shock, we watch as they move slowly and inevitably toward the murder, justifying their choices in any way necessary. They first start to buy clothing, cars, and food on credit. Buildings begin to be renovated, and people seem to be looking forward to better times to come. Meanwhile, sentiment in the town turns from regarding Ill as the favorite for the next mayoral election to seeing him as an object of contempt and hatred. One by one, they turn against him, finally deciding to execute Ill following a public ceremony to accept the gift from Zachanassian. As the press leaves, the leaders of the community surround Ill and strangle him, then head off to the reception, leaving Zachanassian to take her former lover home for burial. *The Visit* is a chilling vision of the lengths people will go to for money—or revenge.

Key Content Areas

Like *The Physicists*, *The Visit* is a sort of modern morality play, basically holding up a mirror to the dark side of human nature. The ability of the townspeople to change their moral compass in the face of Zachanassian's offer is the core issue, clouded by the truth of the accusation against Ill. Ill, in effect, has ruined Zachanassian's life; the issues, however, are whether Claire is really seeking "justice" and the sad pliability of the townspeople.

Potential Connections/Ideas

As a modern morality play, this work makes an interesting pair with Sophocles' play *Antigone*, in which a woman is condemned to death for violating the law, but with extenuating circumstances. A discussion of the similarities and differences between the two cases might make a provocative discussion. Another work in which greed overcomes morality with devastating results is Frank Norris's *McTeague;* its ugliness even surpasses that of *The Visit.* For a more classical take on the precariousness of power and morality, Shakespeare's *Measure for Measure* is an excellent play frequently passed over in the classroom for the more popular *Merchant of Venice.* Toni Morrison's *Song of Solomon* also broaches the morality of some pursuits of "justice." Of course, a teacher could also move to the other Dürrenmatt play reviewed here, *The Physicists,* for a more complex moral issue to debate. Finally, issues of race and morality are involved in the Spike Lee movie *Do the Right Thing,* and the muddy waters surrounding the Crown Heights riots in 1991 are in Anna Deavere Smith's monologue series, *Fires in the Mirror,* also reviewed in this book.

Red Flags

The casually grotesque manner of the townspeople as they throw aside their morals is more disturbing than anything else in this play, but the eunuchs may provoke some immature comments if not handled carefully.

Suggested Grade

The Visit would be readable in any high school classroom, although the moral issues considered might be best discussed by older students.

Film Versions

The Visit. Dir. Bernhard Wicki. With Ingrid Bergman. 1964. B&W, 100 min.

Critical Readings

Olds, Mason. "Ethics and Literature." *The Humanist* 45 (Sept./Oct. 1985): 19–24+. Lays out the ethical issues of *The Visit* from each key character's point of view and argues that such texts are an effective means of provoking thoughtful discourse on what constitutes an ethical decision.

Volpone

1606

Ben Jonson

Characters: 12+ Male; 2 Female
Leads: 10+
Setting: Venice in Jonson's time
Length: Five acts

Synopsis

Volpone begins with the revelation that Volpone, the title character, is in the midst of conning four wealthy gentlepersons out of their money. Each of the four, laboring under the impression that Volpone is dying (a trick devised and carried out with the assistance of Volpone's "parasite," Mosca), brings the wealthy trickster a valuable gift in hopes of securing their place as heir to his fortune with their "generosity." Mosca artfully plays the four off against each other, with each thinking that they have the inside track to the wealth.

When he hears that one of his victims, Corvino, has a lovely wife named Celia, Volpone arranges to see her for himself. Disguised as a mountebank, he sees her standing in her window and at once lusts for her. Mosca helps him to his goal once again, this time convincing the extremely jealous Corvino that he could secure his place in Volpone's frail, dying heart for certain if he would let his wife sleep next to Volpone in a last-ditch attempt to cure him. Persuaded that this treatment prescribed by doctors is harmless (Volpone is too ill and frail to lust), Corvino agrees.

Meanwhile, Volpone and Mosca have also convinced another of the marks, Corbaccio, to disinherit his son Bonario and name Volpone heir—an act that Volpone, Mosca tells Corbaccio, must certainly reciprocate out of gratitude. When Bonario hears of this, he comes to verify the truth himself. Hiding in Volpone's room, he sees Corvino bring his wife Celia in, against her will, to lie with Volpone. As soon at Corvino departs, Volpone is up and protesting his love for Celia. When she rejects his advances, he moves to force her to yield, and Bonario bursts forth to save her. The two escape, threatening to expose Volpone's fraud, but Mosca persuades the four hopefuls to swear to Volpone's illness and to bear false witness against the character of Celia, claiming she and Bonario have had a longstanding affair. The court is moved by the testimony of the four wealthy citizens, including Bonario's father, and orders the innocent pair imprisoned.

Volpone decides to end the farce with the four and, to tweak them, names Mosca his heir and pretends to be dead. The four are distraught that they have lost their gifts and have been double-crossed by Mosca, and they head for court to charge him with fraud. Mosca, meanwhile, as the declared heir, has control of Volpone's home and fortune and decides to blackmail Volpone for half of his wealth. Mosca is brought to court by the four fools and there tries to force Volpone to agree to his terms instead of revealing his secret. Mosca hesitates, and Volpone, fearing that he will lose everything if he does not speak up, reveals himself. The plots are all revealed, and the judges angrily sentence the greedy fools, Mosca, and Volpone to humiliation and imprisonment. Bonario and Celia are freed and rewarded for their honesty, and the deceivers, caught in their own net of lies, lose everything.

Key Content Areas

Jonson's play is a moral comedy. The main characters, with the exceptions of Bonario and Celia, are ethically bankrupt and largely foolish, and through them Jonson attacks the sagging morality of England and its general willingness to put profit and business above honor and ethics. Greed and deception are central, as is the idea that those who indulge in these vices will be hoisted by their own petards, so to speak.

Potential Connections/Ideas

Volpone's biting social satire is a precursor to the work of eighteenth-century writers such as Pope and Swift and could be used with these two authors in a unit on the development of satire in English literature. Pope's *Rape of the Lock* or *The Dunciad* and Swift's *Tale of a Tub* or *Gulliver's Travels* would be ideal for such a study, and they lead naturally to Oscar Wilde's *The Importance of Being Earnest* or Sinclair Lewis's *Elmer Gantry*. Teachers might turn to political cartoons or television for examples of modern satire as well. On a simpler level, *Volpone* can be used to explore symbolism, since the majority of character names reflect the behavior of the character (Volpone means fox, for example).

Jonson's traditional place in the literary canon as the heir to Shakespeare makes a comparison of the styles of the two writers an interesting option. Although not nearly as vicious in its hostility or cynicism as *Volpone*, Shakespeare's *Measure for Measure* is also a story of deception, greed, and abused innocents that ends in the exposure and punishment of those who have done wrong. *The Merchant of Venice* also deals with the willingness of a man to deceive and even kill for the sake of money and vengeance.

Finally, those interested in the use of high comedy as social critique will find several other texts with similar intentions. In the Middle Ages, Chaucer did much the same thing with his witty *Canterbury Tales*, particularly in his treatment of characters such as the Miller, the Friar, and the Pardoner. Both Henry Fielding and Jane Austen used a light tone as cover for social commentary in *Jonathan Wild* and *Northanger Abbey*, respectively. In the twentieth century, authors who stand out as masters of this device include John Updike, John Irving, Kurt Vonnegut, and Tom Wolfe. Students may find it interesting to trace the development of this form from the works of the great Roman satirist Juvenal to the novels of today.

Red Flags

There are a significant number of sexual puns and references, as well as jokes about hermaphrodites. Although no profanity is involved and the lines in question are mostly double-entendres, the strong suggestion of promiscuity in places may be problematic for some school systems.

Suggested Grade

Primarily for seniors, for whom British literature is the usual course of study. *Volpone* is a good example of the biting satires of the seventeenth and eighteenth centuries, and even today it acquits itself well in performance. The characters, while still appearing foolish, are just as recognizable today as they were to Jonson's contemporaries in the audience.

Film Versions

Volpone. Dir. Maurice Tourneur. 1940. B&W, 80 min. French with English subtitles.

The Big Fox. Dir. Maurizio Ponzi. 1988. Italian with English subtitles.

Critical Readings

Bryant, J. A. Jr. *The Compassionate Satirist: Ben Jonson and His Imperfect World.* Athens: University of Georgia P, 1972. Contains background on Jonson's purpose and style and a chapter on *Volpone* in particular, in which Bryant analyzes the weighty nature of *Volpone* as comedy that has led some critics to call it a tragedy.

Waiting for Godot *1948*

Samuel Beckett

Characters: 5 Male; 0 Female
Leads: 4
Setting: A country road, by a tree, sometime in the evening
Length: Two acts

Synopsis

Estragon and Vladimir, two poor men, are waiting for the arrival of an undefined character named Godot. The play itself consists of two acts, each mirroring the last but with an unclear amount of time passing between the two. In each act, Vladimir and Estragon meet in a confused state, unsure of the time that has passed since their last meeting. They remind each other of their purpose—to wait for Godot—then argue over their persistence, their lack of hope, uncertainty regarding their own existences, and even whether they should simply kill themselves, but can come to no decision, so they wait on. In each act, a man named Pozzo appears, holding a rope tied to a man named Lucky. Their appearance, however, changes from act to act, and neither is able to help Vladimir or Estragon break their stasis. At the end of each act, a boy appears, informing the two that Godot will not be coming today but that he is very likely to come tomorrow. In frustration, Vladimir and Estragon agree to leave, but as the curtain closes, they do not move.

Key Content Areas

Waiting for Godot is a play that explores several philosophical questions. Depending on your interests or agenda for the unit, you could discuss the play in terms of religion and religious imagery, as a vision of the human condition and of our day-to-day existence, or as a visual example of the frustrations that modernism tries to express in moving away from all things traditional.

Potential Connections/Ideas

The cyclical construction and empty, barren staging and action of this play are probably unlike anything most students have encountered before and would be a good place to start a discussion of the idea of "exploratory" literature and theater. Some other unusual works that might be brought in include the more playful oddities of David

Ives's *Sure Thing* or *Phillip Glass Buys a Loaf of Bread,* Don DeLillo's postmodern novel *White Noise,* or Pirandello's *Six Characters in Search of an Author.*

More advanced classes may decide to take on the deeper questions inherent in *Waiting for Godot,* such as why we exist and what we are striving for. Who is our personal Godot, or do we have one at all? The religious implications of Vladimir's first act foray into discussions of the gospel and of "waiting for Godot" in general provoked excellent discussions in my eleventh-grade class. One could further such a discussion (as we did) by turning to other works that deal with our purpose and our desires, such as Kurt Vonnegut's *Breakfast of Champions,* or examine Shakespeare's "All the world's a stage" metaphor with a bridge to Tom Stoppard's *Rosencrantz and Guildenstern Are Dead,* or bring in a classical point of view with Samuel Johnson's easily readable novel *Rasselas.* In any case, I highly recommend reading and rereading this play out loud as the unit progresses; we found that repeated hearings had a major effect on our interpretations.

Red Flags

The word *bastard* crops up a few times, but not much else beyond the references to venereal disease.

Suggested Grade

Waiting for Godot is a tough play that requires patient, mature students. It is best suited for eleventh- or twelfth-graders or perhaps a very advanced tenth-grade class.

Film Versions

Waiting for Godot. With Brian Blessed and Leslie Grantham. 1991.

Critical Readings

Calderwood, James L. "Ways of Waiting in *Waiting for Godot.*" *Modern Drama* 29 (Sept. 1986): 363–75. A very detailed and thorough analysis of the "waiting" motif in Beckett's play. The language of the essay is academic but mostly readable.

Cousineau, Thomas J. *Waiting for Godot: Form in Movement.* Boston: Twayne, 1990. A short book examining the play in depth, with chapters on the themes of Christianity, truth, language, causality, memory, and friendship, among others. Includes a bibliography.

Nealon, Jeffrey. "Samuel Beckett and the Postmodern: Language Games, Play, and *Waiting for Godot.*" *Modern Drama* 31 (Dec. 1988): 520–28. A critical analysis of Beckett's use of wordplay to designate a Wittgenstein-style discourse community based on language play. For readers familiar with the postmodern critical framework (for example, Derrida, Wittgenstein, and Lyotard) only.

Worton, Michael. "*Waiting for Godot* and *Endgame:* Theatre as Text." *The Cambridge Companion to Beckett.* Ed. John Pilling. New York: Cambridge University P, 1994. 67–85. A moderately difficult essay regarding the philosophical and biblical underpinnings of the two plays. Postulates that the characters in each play need each other to prove their existence to themselves, as much as for any other purpose.

Waiting for Lefty

1935

Clifford Odets

Characters: 13 Male; 2 Female
Leads: 15
Setting: A bare stage, representing the stage at a taxicab drivers' union meeting, 1935
Length: Full play

Synopsis

Waiting for Lefty is a series of flashback vignettes that occur as stories told by speakers at a union meeting. The meeting opens with the union's head, Harry Fatt, addressing the crowd from the stage. He is surrounded by a committee of workers and has some hired muscle—a gunman—on the stage with him as well. Fatt argues against striking, first claiming that a strike would hurt FDR, a man he says is standing for labor. When the other members begin to object, he calls them communists and threatens them. A call for Lefty goes up, and Fatt quickly agrees. Where is Lefty? he asks. He ought to be here, and he's obviously run out on you.

One of the union members, angry at Fatt's comments and his position, takes the stage and begins to argue in favor of a strike. We need a living wage, he says, and the scene then cuts to a flashback. We watch as Joe, the speaker, comes home to find his furniture repossessed, his children missing meals, and his wife threatening to leave him because he's not providing for her or their children. He tries to argue that a strike will cost him his job, but she points out that losing his job is meaningless if he can't survive with it. He argues that he's just one man, but she points out that he's part of a union and that there are hundreds in the union. What has it done for him so far but take his dues? She presses Joe to demand action, or she'll leave him. Joe is galvanized by the force of her demands, and heads off to find Lefty. The flashback ends, and Joe takes his seat, his address to the crowd finished.

Another vignette unfolds next, this time involving an industrialist and a lab assistant. The industrialist offers the lab assistant a raise, then a new position in an important lab. Of course, the lab assistant will have to live at the lab during the time he'll be working, but his wife will certainly understand. The lab assistant expresses qualms about the products being made for use in warfare, but the industrialist dismisses them as irrelevant. He then tells the lab assistant that he'll want a weekly report on the progress the lab is making—confidentially. The lab assistant, realizing he's being asked to spy on his fellow workers, refuses. The industrialist threatens the assistant with firing for defying him, but the man stands his ground, accepting that he's lost his job for his principles but easing his pain by getting in one good punch to the mouth of the industrialist.

The next vignette shows two young lovers, Florence and Sid. They clearly love each other, and they clearly want to marry, but it isn't possible on Sid's salary, and both know it. The scene ends with the two weeping as they end their romance.

Fatt now takes the stage to argue against the need for a strike. He brings in a man he claims is a union man from Philadelphia, a victim of the last strike movement, but the man is quickly exposed by his brother, who is in the audience, as an informant who breaks unions by infiltrating them and providing lists of members for blacklisting. He's chased off the stage to make room for the next vignette, a short piece in which a doctor finds that he is being cut from the hospital he works for because he's Jewish. He, too, seeks some sort of labor movement to try to make a change.

The vignette ends, and a man named Agate is the last speaker on the stage. He sums up what has been said—that the union leaders have been bought, that the union members want a working wage, and that the only way that they can keep their pride and their lives is to strike. As he urges the crowd to a frenzy, a man runs in with the news that Lefty has been found shot to death near the taxi garages. The play ends with the room erupting with chants of "Strike! Strike!"

Key Content Areas

Waiting for Lefty is a fiercely pro-union play that condemns the injustice of the capitalist culture of the early twentieth century. By showing the way that injustice hurts employees at all levels—taxicab drivers, white collar managers, lab workers, and even doctors—Odets hopes to galvanize public support for laws to protect the rights of workers.

Potential Connections/Ideas

As a social protest play, *Waiting for Lefty* fits well with other works that deal with the injustices faced by a segment of the population and the difficulties in remedying the situation. Upton Sinclair's *The Jungle,* Charles Dickens's *Hard Times,* and Eugene O'Neill's *The Hairy Ape* all focus on the plight of the working class in an industrial society. *A Raisin in the Sun,* by Lorraine Hansberry, and *Fences,* by August Wilson, also look at the same issues but from the perspective of African American families. Teachers developing a more general unit on literature as social critique might begin with Chaucer's *Canterbury Tales* and proceed to works such as Jonathan Swift's *Gulliver's Travels,* Mark Twain's *The Innocents Abroad,* and Bertold Brecht's *The Three-Penny Opera.*

The unusual construction of *Waiting for Lefty* may also offer opportunities to work it into a classroom curriculum. Teachers looking for examples of a variety of styles of dramatic presentation should also look at Anna Deavere Smith's extended use of monologues in *Fires in the Mirror,* Pirandello's destruction of conventions in *Six Characters in Search of an Author,* Samuel Beckett's highly experimental short plays, or the exploration of the variety of possibilities in any single meeting seen in David Ives's one-act play *Sure Thing.* Even the "waiting" motif of *Waiting for Godot* and the question of paralysis versus action could be used to build a connection between Beckett's philosophical play and Odets's more political work.

Red Flags

Several racial epithets. In one case, the slang used by the industrialist underscores his view of workers as subhuman chattel to be bought and sold. In another, the epithet is used to underscore the fondness of the speaker for the character in question. The words used, however, are no worse than those found in *Huckleberry Finn,* and if taught with the same care to explain that the terms are unacceptable for common usage, should pose no more an obstacle to teaching this play than to teaching Twain's classic.

Suggested Grade

Eleventh grade and up. Odets's stirring condemnation of social injustice is best suited for inclusion in a course on American literature or as part of a team-taught American history unit, both common as junior year courses of study.

Appendix A
A Sample Unit Plan

Shakespeare's *Macbeth* Integrated with Arthur Miller's *Death of a Salesman*

This unit plan is an example of integration of drama into the English classroom. I've chosen a plan involving *Macbeth* because of its almost sacrosanct position in the twelfth-grade curriculum. Pairing *Macbeth* with *Death of a Salesman* allows teachers two opportunities for flexibility. First, the teacher can break up the linear path often followed from Old English to modern literature, a path that covers much of the most difficult material in the first half of the school year. *Death of a Salesman* is a modern, easy-to-follow companion piece that can highlight the elements of tragedy. Second, the teacher can focus on the development of the tragic hero and the changes to the genre over the past four hundred years and make historical connections outside the English class.

The assignments in this unit offer a variety of assessment forms to embrace the differences we find in classrooms today. They include creative, oral, and written work, as well as alternatives for students unwilling to involve themselves directly in performance work. When you design your own plans, remember that the reason you are incorporating drama into your classroom is to offer more opportunities for inclusion and engagement. Designing assessment opportunities in a number of areas allows more students opportunities to excel.

A: *Macbeth*

1. Introduction to Elizabethan theater
2. Discussion of methods of acting
3. Read Act 1
4. Outline characters and plot
5. Read Act 2
6. Discussion and analysis: *Macbeth* as tragedy
7. Read Act 3
8. Optional activity: director's exercises in stage plotting
9. Discussion: Macbeth's conscience
10. Optional reading: excerpts from Ionesco's *Macbett*
11. Small group performance assignments
12. Read Act 4
13. Stagework
14. Group rehearsal day
15. Read Act 5

16. Assessment: in-class writing assignment
17. Small group performances
18. Closing discussion: Is Macbeth a tragic hero?

B: *Death of a Salesman*

1. Introduction: Arthur Miller and the modern theater
2. Read Act 1
3. Outline characters and plot
4. Discussion: Willy Loman, weak protagonist or tragic hero?
5. Read Act 2
6. Assessment: Macbeth versus Willy Loman trial activity
7. Closing discussion: the transition from Macbeth to Willy Loman as tragic hero

A: *Macbeth*

1. Introduction to Elizabethan Theater

Objective: Students will learn about the design of an Elizabethan theater and the rules of the Elizabethan stage.

Method: Lecture

Key Points

- *Design of the Globe Theater:* Three-tiered, arena-style theater with thrust stage. Seating in boxes and standing room in "the pit." Stage constructed with earthen ramps leading to the pit, which led to occasional problems with spectators storming the stage. Stage seating was eventually added, where spectators could sit on stools on the edge of the action. This was considered a place of high honor. Building or pavilion located at the rear of the stage as a semi-permanent structure (extent of permanence depending on scholar consulted). The stage level of this building contained two large doors that led to the inner portion of the building, known as the "discovery space." Atop the first level was a second area, partially set up as balcony, and behind it a second "discovery space." Above this level was a small musicians' gallery. Not much space for storage or changing; actors sometimes rented changing rooms in buildings next to the theater.
- *Stage rules:* Minimal scenery meant that scenes were largely set up by directly stating the locale early in the scene. Standardized sets were common (castle, clearing, bedroom) and could be set up in advance, with discovery spaces serving as short transition scene rooms. No lighting; shows were held during the day, and night scenes were set up by carrying in torches or talking about how dark it was. Some sound effects (for example, lightning and thunder) were available.
- *Costuming:* The most complicated part of theater was costuming. Five different costume styles existed: "ancient" (out of style or unfashionable), "antique" (clas-

sical figure), "fanciful" (ghosts and goblins, etc.), "traditional" (specific characters such as Robin Hood or Falstaff), "national or racial" (denoting Jews, Turks, Spaniards, Indians, and so on). Costuming consumed large portions of the company budget.

- *Audience:* Drawn in by flags and handbills. Capacity in an average theater is estimated at 1,500 to 2,500, and theaters were usually half-full for most performances. Plays were regularly rotated and added to the bill. Play started around 2 P.M. Pit standing room was a penny, gallery seating two pence, and box seating three pence and up. By the seventeenth century, prices had risen to two pence for general admission and up to twenty pence for a box. Prices could be raised for special shows and doubled for premieres. All classes attended the theater.
- *Actors:* All male. Troupe was about ten to twenty-five people; shows were double-cast regularly. More than half the troupe were "hired men" who earned salaries similar to skilled laborers. Others included apprentices, boys who were in training with established actors. These boys started as young as six years old and were made full actors as late as eighteen or twenty-one years old. Best pay went to shareholders in the company—older members who would get more shares as a bonus for long-term service to the company. Shares were used to divide profits from performance and to ensure loyalty to the company.

Dramatic Form (Tragedy): Outline the five-act model for dramatic development in a tragedy. The action follows a roller-coaster style arc. In acts 1 and 2, characters are introduced and the conflict that will drive the plot is unveiled. In Act 3, the plot and characters are developed, and direct movement toward the climax of the action begins. The audience is presented with twists, reversals, or small climactic moments to increase tension. In Act 4, the equivalent of the top of the roller-coaster's hill, the final conflict becomes clear, as does the path that the climax will follow. In Act 5, we plunge to the conclusion as rapidly as possible to maintain the audience's interest and focus. This approach optimally produces the catharsis sought in tragedy.

Assessment: Ask students to "cast" and "set" modern TV shows or movie scenes in Elizabethan stage form. Use responses to check understanding.

2. Discussion of Methods of Acting

Objective: Students will learn some basic rules of acting and be able to apply them to their readings. Students will practice these methods.

Method: Model and practice.

- Explain to students the difference between reading and acting. Encourage students to define *acting.*
- Show students that acting is actually a large part of our daily lives. Point out to students that they act when they tell stories to a group of friends, when they try to convince a parent to give them an extra hour on the curfew, or when they tell teachers, "It'll be in tomorrow." Encourage students by telling them that

stage acting will feel natural to them once they break through the barrier of the "audience."

- Talk about what actors have to do with characters: Think about motivation, character, and behavior. How does the character really look? Stand? Walk? Talk? Is the character a good guy? Bad guy? How can you tell? Get students to explain that the actor reads the play and then makes decisions on how to portray the character based on the character's interactions with other characters, speeches, and internal monologues. Most important is to get students to acknowledge that the actor takes part in the creative process, making the character whole. The author doesn't provide all the material but only sketches. An actor must make the character come alive.
- Go over basic stage directions from *Macbeth*, making sure that students can distinguish between action and dialogue and that students get into the habit of reading past line breaks for stage directions to ensure that students don't cut lines.

Practice: Use improvisation games to practice basic acting skills and to break down resistance to acting in public. Get student volunteers for games in which the audience gives two characters emotions and the characters must act a scene using the emotions or games in which the audience has to guess what the character is playing or doing.

Alternative Activity for Reluctant or Nonparticipatory Students: Ask students to write one-page character sketches for TV or movie characters, outlining a typical day for the character and giving personal information (favorite color, snack food, etc.). Try to avoid this assignment if at all possible. This unit will work best if all students participate, so alternatives should be used only if a student is about to storm out of the class rather than do the acting.

3. Read Act 1

4. Outline Characters and Plot

Objective: Ensure that students have a clear picture of the relationships between the characters and the roles of each character in the drama and that the basic plot is understood.

Method: I prefer question and answer here, to try to get students to reinforce their own reading. Supplement with lecture as necessary.

- As an additional activity, ask students to predict what will happen to the characters they've seen so far and what role they may play in the action to come. Discuss the reasons for their educated guesses. Ask students who suggest Duncan is going to be killed what they think will keep the play moving after the king dies.

5. Read Act 2

6. Discussion and Analysis: *Macbeth* as Tragedy

Objective: Students will consider the definition of tragedy and discuss whether *Macbeth* fits the pattern at this point. Students then decide what must happen for *Macbeth* to fit in the genre.

Method: Discussion. Ask students to define *tragedy* (in the dramatic sense); write working definitions on the board and refine them through leading questions until some consensus is reached. Most students will view *Macbeth* as falling outside the traditional boundaries of tragedy because Macbeth's actions evoke little sympathy early in the play. Some students, however, may point out that *Macbeth* is a tragedy because we watch a great man (Macbeth) succumb to temptation and poor decisions, eventually leading to his destruction—the same pattern seen in classic tragedies such as *Oedipus Rex.*

Regardless of what consensus students reach, continue by asking them what sorts of things must happen in the remaining acts of the play to ensure that Shakespeare's work ends as a tragedy. Students should recognize that for the tragedy to be effective, we must at some point begin to feel some sympathy for Macbeth. How might Shakespeare make us feel sorry for a man who kills his own king?

7. Read Act 3

8. Optional Activity: Director's Exercises in Stage Plotting

Note: This exercise assumes that the teacher has a minimal familiarity with stage plots or directing notes. If you are not, this may be an ideal time to get to know your school's drama teacher. Ask him or her to come in and talk about staging, or just ask to see a few of the stage diagrams from the last show they directed. If you don't believe that you can teach this material effectively, cut this section. It is optional, and no damage will be done to the unit as a whole.

Objective: Students will begin to think like directors, setting up stage plots and identifying and making performance choices. Students will successfully create stage plots for a scene. Students will recognize that they are becoming active partners in literature, not passive readers.

Method

- Draw a trapezoid (stage shape) on the chalkboard. Walk students through the composition of a stage plot with a scene that they are familiar with. Explain how a stage plot shows scenery pieces, entrances, and location of actors to start and then maps out the movement during the scene. Note that there is no "correct" way to plot; the goal is to create a plot that is clear and consistent. I use letters to identify characters (M = Macbeth, LM = Lady Macbeth, MD = Macduff, etc.) and arrows to indicate movement.

- Give students another scene to work with. Ask them to compose their own stage plot by using the same technique. Remind them that all actors and scenery must be clearly marked to prevent confusion and that the plot should be easily read by others.
- Ask students to share their stage plots by drawing them on the board. Review several of the plots by having actors walk through the action as scripted in the plot. Use walkthroughs to get the class to critique the effectiveness of each plot and discuss the alternatives open to them.
- Once they have narrowed the plots down to the viable ones, ask them which plot works best. Remind them that they need to take into account where the characters were at the end of the last scene that they exited from and that it is always easiest if the next entrance for a character comes from the same side of the stage as his or her last exit. Talk about effective motion and dead time and how to minimize conflicting paths on stage.
- Conclude with a discussion of active and passive reading. Explain that as students are learning to identify and make performance choices, they are creating their own version of *Macbeth*, a version just as valid as any professional production. Emphasize the importance of their role as active readers in both creating and preserving literature.

Assessment: Stage plots produced by the students can be used to assess their progress toward director's thinking. Progress toward "outside the box" thinking should be noticeable in writing assignments as students learn that they can experiment with undefined variables in a text.

No alternative assignment should be necessary for this segment of the unit.

9. Discussion: Macbeth's Conscience

Objective: Students will examine material in acts 1 to 3 to illuminate the question of Macbeth's conscience.

Method: Individual work and discussion. Ask students to identify passages in which Macbeth wrestles with his conscience (I.7.1–28, II.1.33–64, II.2, and III.1 are all good examples). How does it affect him before and after the death of King Duncan? What signs have we seen that Macbeth is changing? What convinces him to proceed? Does he show true remorse or merely a hardening of purpose?

10. Optional Reading: Excerpts from Ionesco's *Macbett*

Objective: Students will read portions of Eugene Ionesco's *Macbett*, a rewritten version of Shakespeare's *Macbeth*. They will consider the purpose of Ionesco's parody and assess its effectiveness. Students will discuss the lines between adaptation, rewriting, and making directorial choices.

Method: Provide students with short (one to three scenes) excerpts of Ionesco's version of the *Macbeth* story. Read the work silently or aloud, as desired. Ask students the differences between the two works. What do those differences tell us about the intentions of each author? Is *Macbett* about the crisis of conscience one man undergoes, like *Macbeth*? What does Ionesco gain by parodying *Macbeth*? Does it help him make his point? How?

- How many changes does a director have to make before a play is no longer the play the author intended? Does a director have the right to alter stage directions or lines that an author specifies? Is there any sort of guideline a director might follow as to what is permitted and what is going too far?

11. Small Group Performance Assignments

Objective: Students will synthesize lessons learned earlier in the unit as they break into small groups and select scenes to examine in depth and perform. Students will increase their confidence in their understanding of the text and their right to an interpretation through active performance.

Method

- Instruct students that they are to spend the next few minutes choosing scenes that they will rehearse for performance before the class. The scene should contain roughly twenty lines of material for each character; students may stop a longer scene at a reasonable break in the action to keep the line count reasonable. The students should be told that the primary criterion for their scene choice should be an understanding of the action in that scene, as they will need to convey the emotions of the characters in their performances. I strongly encourage teachers to insist that students try to memorize their parts in the scene; acting with a script in hand is virtually impossible for new actors. Students should decide among themselves which scenes have the best potential and then gather into groups appropriate in size. Make sure all students are accounted for, and have some scenes available for the inevitable "I don't know what scene I should do."
- *Alternative Assignment for Nonparticipatory Students:* Assign such students the role of stage manager. That student is responsible for all sound effects and props to be used in each scene, setting up the stage, and handing out scripts. Assignments for this student might include sketching set designs for key scenes, costuming suggestions, lighting and sound effects lists for full productions, and learning how to operate light and sound boards in the main auditorium, under supervision, for use during stage work section.
- Break into scene groups. On group rehearsal day, each group will get a part of the period as "stage time," when they can be working on walkthroughs and positioning. The remainder of the work time will be spent practicing reading in small groups, writing up scene plots, and discussing interpretations. Make sure students are aware that they have limited time to work on this project (Act 4 and

stagework usually require three to five classes total) and that they should be working on their lines at home as well as in any rehearsal time you provide or that they arrange out of school.

- As performance day moves near, require each group to submit a written summary of the scene they are going to perform. Stage plots should also be submitted, and groups should arrange for all props and costumes they want to use. This allows you to verify that the group understands the material they are presenting and forces them to consider motivations of characters and the emotional state of each at the time of the scene.

12. Read Act 4

13. Stagework

Objective: Students will experience stage performance and learn the difference between small and large space acting. Students will learn to use available space to best advantage. Students will increase their comfort level of public speaking through the culmination of a gradual increase in "on-stage" awareness. Students will gain increased appreciation of the text through stagework.

Method

- Meet class in the theater. Have lights preset on full first day. Bring the students up on stage and ask them to walk around. Sit down at center stage and talk about how it feels. Look out at the audience, and point out how it's almost impossible to see people against the stage lights. Show students backstage areas. Emphasize how this is now their stage to work with. For many students, this will be the first time they've been on a stage; make it a positive experience.
- Begin by staying on stage with students. Read a key scene aloud, assigning parts as needed; then ask students to try walking through the scene. Encouragement is vital at this stage.
- Second class: Begin to break down dependence on group presence as support. Have students who are in the scene stay in the scene while students who aren't in the scene are in the wings watching. Explain the idea of visibility and angles, and make sure students stay "invisible." If there is a "stage manager" in the class, position that student in the tech booth with a headset so that light levels can be adjusted as appropriate. Care should be taken to make sure this student remains part of the class; using him or her as an audibility check is helpful, and this student should always know what page and line of a scene the actors are on and be ready to prompt. Making it clear that this effort is part of the student's unit grade will help ensure engagement.
- Third and fourth classes: Take students who are not in the scene off the stage. Students should become familiar with acting for an audience. Continue to encourage refinement of acting skills. Begin to bring in props and small set pieces

(black boxes, etc.) to give students a true acting feel. Spend time on movement and "stage presence"; explain that large motions are necessary to be visible to audience. Exaggeration is encouraged. Teach students voice projection, or some simple diction exercises, such as repeating the phrase "red leather yellow leather good blood bad blood" quickly but precisely.

14. Group Rehearsal Day(s)

Method: Set aside at least one day for student groups to practice for their performance. If the stage is available, make sure each group gets a reasonable portion of the period to rehearse there (fifteen minutes as a minimum). If not, secure permission to spread out into multiple rooms or outside areas to obtain the necessary space for group work. Circulate from group to group; be sure to offer positive feedback on their efforts as well as suggestions for improvement.

15. Read Act 5

16. Assessment: In-Class Writing Assignment

Objective: Students will demonstrate comprehension of the play *Macbeth* by writing a short essay in class.

Method: Ask students to write a five-paragraph essay on a topic that draws on previously discussed ideas. Two examples:

  a. Who is the more evil character, Macbeth or Lady Macbeth? Why?
  b. Explain how Shakespeare uses imagery to show Macbeth's increasing evil.

17. Small Group Performances

Objective: Students will synthesize lessons learned in previous units as they perform a prepared scene.

Method

- On performance day, each group should perform their scene for the remainder of the class. Invite other classes or administrators to watch the performances.
- After all performances are complete, have a group discussion of this part of the unit. Did students feel comfortable in interpreting the material? Were they comfortable directing their own scenes? Why or why not? Which interpretations would Shakespeare have approved of? Why? Does it matter? Why or why not?

Assessment: Performance, along with the stage plots and written summaries turned in earlier.

18. Closing Discussion: Is Macbeth a Tragic Hero?

Objective: Assess students' comprehension of the unit material. Students will be able to answer this question thoughtfully and use examples from the text to support their position.

Method: Discussion. Ask students to consider all the evidence regarding Macbeth's conscience, particularly his final scenes. Does Macbeth redeem himself to some extent by dying in combat? Does his regret late in the play or the suicide of his wife earn him sympathy?

- On a broader note, ask students what they think has made *Macbeth* endure over time. Can we identify in any way with Macbeth or with other characters in the play? Are we meant to? Would people in Shakespeare's day be more or less likely to identify with Macbeth? Why?

B: *Death of a Salesman*

1. Introduction: Arthur Miller and the Modern Theater

Objective: Students will learn important background information on realism and Arthur Miller's vision of the tragedy.

Method: Lecture.

- Arthur Miller grew up in a middle-class family and was exposed early to the ups and downs of the working world. He distinguished himself early on as a play-wright but tried to live a simple life away from the intellectual circles of his day. Born in 1916, he experienced the era of the WPA, World War II, and the cold war; each left a mark on his literary career. His fondness for the average working man can be seen in *Death of a Salesman;* his frustration with the McCarthy hearings and the Communist witch-hunts of the 1950s is clearly visible in *The Crucible.*
- Miller's theory of drama was simple. He argued that the only honest drama is drama taken from real-life experiences and dealing with moral issues. In his works, Miller tries to capture a slice of reality, forcing his characters to face difficult choices to do what is right. This often forces ordinary people into the type of Herculean effort that Miller believed allowed them to attain tragic hero status.
- To Miller, even the average person could be a tragic hero if he or she struggled hard enough. The key, he believed, was that a tragic hero holds a vision of herself or himself and is unwilling to release that vision. Tragic heroes fear the loss of that vision; if they cease to believe in themselves, they are in danger of being destroyed by the reality of their own weaknesses or failures.
- Realism: Simply put, a movement in literature and drama that sought to reflect the realities of the time, including working-class characters, plots focusing on the problems of the average person, and carefully written stage directions designed to increase consistency between and precision within performances. Sets became more substantial in construction and less abstract in design, and actors were expected to strictly observe the "fourth wall" convention.

2. Read Act 1

3. Outline Characters and Plot

Objective: Ensure that students have a clear picture of the relationships between the characters and the roles of each character in the drama and that the basic plot is understood.

Method: I prefer question and answer here to try to get students to reinforce their own reading. Supplement with lecture as necessary.

- As an additional activity, ask students to predict what will happen to the characters they've seen so far and what role they may play in the action to come. Discuss the reasons for their educated guesses. In a realist play, we would also expect the sons of a character to echo him in some way. How do Happy and Biff resemble Willy? How do they differ?

4. Discussion: Willy Loman, Weak Protagonist or Tragic Hero?

Objective: Students will debate the merits of Arthur Miller's concept of tragedy and its execution in the character of Willy Loman.

Method: Discussion. Begin by reviewing the traditional definition of tragic hero and the definition Arthur Miller proposes. Which is the more appropriate definition? Do you agree with Miller that average people can achieve tragic status by struggling to rise above their station, even if they fail? If so, does Willy Loman actually struggle to overcome his situation? Does he succeed? Does he elevate himself in the eyes of the reader to tragic hero, or does his refusal to see his own weaknesses make him appear pathetic rather than tragic?

5. Read Act 2

6. Assessment: Macbeth versus Willy Loman Trial Activity

Objective: Students will compare Willy Loman and Macbeth by conducting a mock trial, in which students dispute which character is more culpable in the events of their lives.

Method: Assign two teams of four students each to act as lawyers for Loman and Macbeth. The students may volunteer, or you might use random drawing. Assign remaining students to act as "witnesses"—characters from each play the lawyers can call to the stand to testify—and as the main characters. A jury of at least five students should be assigned as well.

Allow the "lawyers" two or three nights to prepare questions. Explain that they will be scored based on the questions they ask and the effectiveness of their arguments. Characters should spend the evenings prior to the trial reviewing their lines in the play to familiarize themselves with the material they will be questioned on. Characters will be scored based on their performance on the stand and their familiarity with their history. Jurors do not have to prepare in advance, but they must write a one- or two-page "judgment" paper following the trial. You may wish to have the jurors read their papers when the votes are tallied, or you may ask them to summarize their reasons for siding one way or the other.

7. Closing Discussion: The Transition from Macbeth to Willy Loman as Tragic Hero

Objective: Students will review the material covered in *Macbeth* and *Death of a Salesman*, with particular emphasis on the concept of tragic hero.

Method: Discussion. What makes *Macbeth* a tragedy? What makes *Death of a Salesman* tragic? Does tragedy come from characters, plot, or both?

Macbeth was a character who would have appeared far above the station of the average theatergoer in the Renaissance. The play itself dealt with intrigue in the court of Scotland, a far cry from the daily drudgery of the peasant. Willy Loman, by contrast, is an average man who lives an average life. His world is similar to ours, and his job is one that many students have held. If realism theorizes that audiences will be more engaged when they watch material that relates directly to their world, what has changed since the Renaissance? Has the audience changed in a significant way that would account for its desire for greater realism? Or is the realist movement mistaken in its assessment of what the modern audience wants?

Appendix B
The "Unit Bull's-eye"

A Complete Set of Ready-to-Use Exercises for Evaluation and Expansion

The goal of an outstanding teacher should always be to provide a variety of activities for assessment. Ideally, students should have equal opportunities to work in areas where they have talent and to stretch their abilities in areas where they need improvement. It is therefore incumbent on us as teachers to supplement the traditional forms of assessment, such as worksheets and essays, with alternate assignments that highlight other skills, such as visual, musical, artistic, or interpersonal verbal methods of interpretation and analysis.

To produce this diversity of assessment, I use a three-part system for assessing one major project a semester. These activities do not replace analytical essays as the primary evaluative exercise in my classroom; our purpose is to prepare the students for the future, and that means preparing them to think and write well. Nevertheless, we should aim to educate the whole student, not just the student writer, and these activities can engage students who are less enthusiastic about traditional assignments.

Each student is required to choose one activity to complete from each of the three areas, reading and reporting (comprehension), creative response, and analytical assignments. I generally weight all three assignments equally.

Reading and Reporting (Comprehension)	Creative Response	Analytical Assignments
"Special Report" Journalistic Writing	"Revision" of One Act	Compare or Contrast Essay
"Events Cards" Challenge	Staged Performance	Scene Presentation or Interpretation
Summary notecards	Videotaped Performance	Character Analysis Essay (Kiersey Temperament Sorter)
Worksheets and Comprehension Quizzes and/or Test	Set Design	
	Soundtrack	
	Comic Book	

To illustrate to students that these skills are interrelated and build on one another, I designed the evaluation bull's-eye (see Figure B.1). The bull's-eye places each of these sets of skills in a ring on the target, and students must complete an assignment from each ring to complete the unit. One benefit of this organizer is that it allows me to easily keep track of which assignments have been completed by each student; I can always require students to complete assignments they haven't attempted in the past if I want them to try to expand their horizons. These exercises can be copied and adapted for your classroom as you see fit.

FIGURE B.1   Ring Assignments for Bull's-eye Unit

Name: _____   Section: _____

Unit Assignment Checksheet

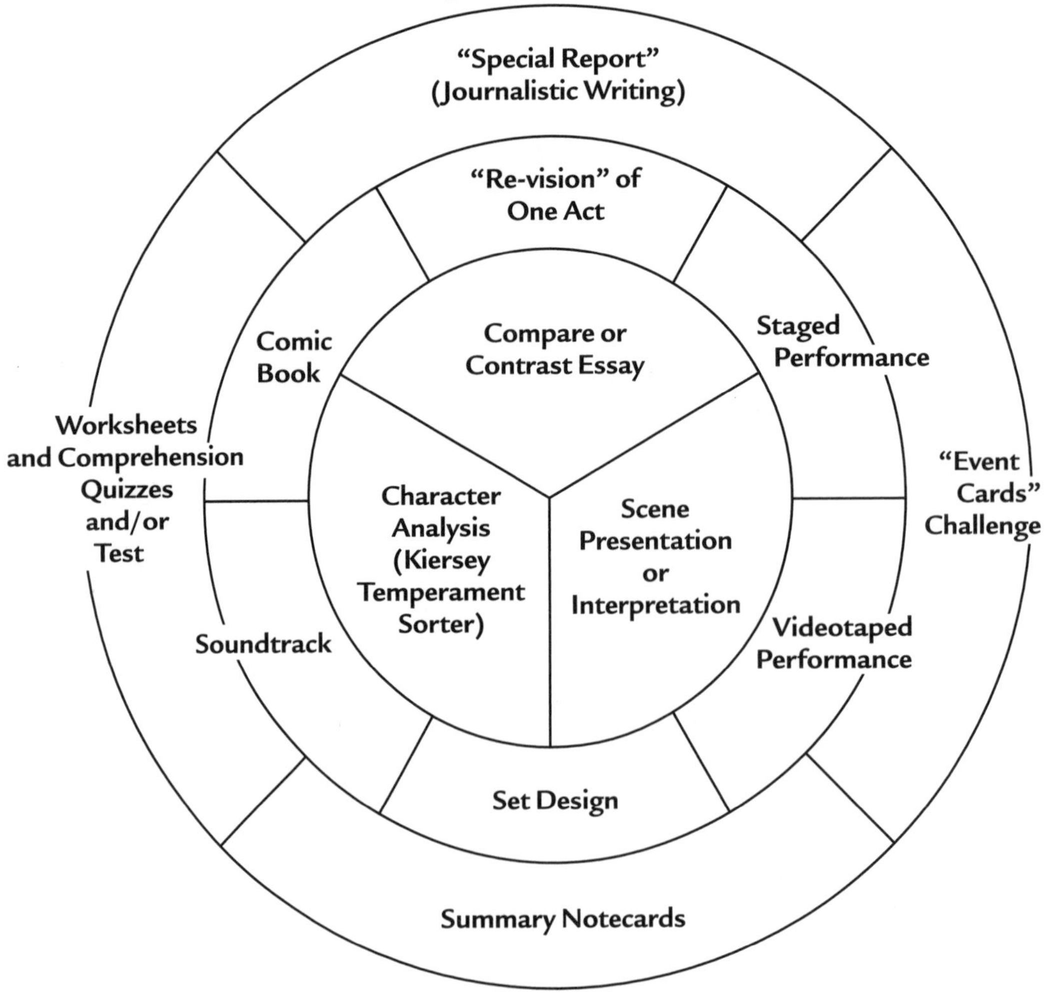

- "Special Report" (Journalistic Writing)
- "Re-vision" of One Act
- Comic Book
- Compare or Contrast Essay
- Staged Performance
- Worksheets and Comprehension Quizzes and/or Test
- Character Analysis (Kiersey Temperament Sorter)
- Scene Presentation or Interpretation
- "Event Cards" Challenge
- Soundtrack
- Videotaped Performance
- Set Design
- Summary Notecards

Ring One Score: _____   Ring Two Score: _____   Ring Three Score: _____   Total Unit Points: _____

Ring One Assignment Guidelines

Reading and Reporting (Comprehension)

"Special Report" (Journalistic Writing)

For this assignment, choose two important events in the text you are studying. Each event should be a critical moment in the story that advances the plot significantly.

1. Begin by rereading one of the sections of the text you plan to work with. Make sure you understand what happens and why it is important. Why do the characters behave the way they do? What events led up to this moment in the story?
2. After you are certain that you understand the material, write a short outline for a news story reporting the events. Remember to answer the critical questions for a good journalist:

    a. What happened?
    b. Where did it happen?
    c. When did it happen?
    d. Who was involved?
    e. Why did it happen?
    f. What may happen as a result?

3. Write the news story in your best journalistic prose. Your job is to present an interesting and informative summary of the events taking place and what led up to them, and to do so in an unbiased manner. Pick an appropriate headline. If possible, use suitable quotes from the text to add realism to your report. Your story should be no less than a page long and no more than two pages long. It will be evaluated on thoroughness, accuracy, and style.
4. Repeat this process for the second story. Turn in neat copies of each story to receive credit for this assignment.

"Event Cards" Challenge

In this assignment, create a set of cards that list the major events of the novel or play you are working with. You will then use the cards to review the story line in preparation for a quiz on the plot. To complete this assignment, you need a pack of twenty-five index cards, of any size.

1. Begin by reviewing the plot of your novel or play. Make sure you understand all the major events in the story; if you have any questions, ask your teacher or a fellow student for assistance.
2. List on paper all the major events of the story that you can think of. One way to come up with these events is to break the text into five equal sections, such as acts of a play or clusters of chapters, and find at least five events in each section to record. Examples may include:

    a. The first time we meet a major character
    b. The protagonist deciding on a course of action
    c. A character falling in love
    d. A birth or death
    e. A fight or argument
    f. The protagonist learning an important piece of information
    g. The discovery of a previously unknown secret

3. Expand your list until it reaches at least twenty-five events. If you have more than twenty-five, choose the twenty-five most important events from the list.
4. Once you have a final list, copy each event on an index card of its own. Be sure *not* to number the cards or to put chapter, act, or page numbers on them. Write down only the event itself. Keep the cards in order for now, but turn in the list to your teacher.
5. After you have completed your deck of cards, read them over carefully. Use them to learn the order of the events; you may wish to practice telling the story yourself by using the cards as reminders.
6. When you feel confident that you know the story well, take the cards to your teacher. The teacher will shuffle the cards and then present you with the shuffled deck. You will then sort the cards into their proper order.

Your grade on this assignment will be based on the accuracy of your sorted cards in step 6, and on your choice of events from the play or novel to use (the list you provided in step 4).

Summary Notecards

For this assignment, you are to prepare a set of summary notecards for the text you have chosen. You will need several 4 × 6 or larger index cards, one for each act of the play or chapter of the novel you chose, plus one extra card for general information. Be neat! Your cards should be easy to read and without errors.

1. Label your first card with the name of the text and the words *General Information*. Underneath, you should include the following information:

    a. Author
    b. Date of publication
    c. A list of the main characters and a description of each one
    d. The setting (time and place) of the text
    e. The major conflict or problem that drives the story

2. On your next card, print the name of the text and *Chapter 1* or *Act 1*. First, list the most important event that occurs in the act or chapter and explain its significance. Next, summarize the action in that section of the text, providing at least a paragraph of information.
3. Repeat this process for the remaining chapters or acts of the text.

4. When you've completed all the cards, arrange them in order. Then check them over to make sure you haven't missed anything important. When you read through the cards, you should have a complete summary of the text from beginning to end.

Ring Two Assignment Guidelines
Creative Response

"Re-vision" of One Act

In this assignment, you are expected to take a single act of the play you are working with or a chapter of the novel you are reading and re-create it in another form. This is a "re-vision" exercise because you are expected to see in your mind's eye an alternate version of the text and then capture that vision on paper. Don't worry too much about what the author's original intent for the text was; instead, ask yourself how you could make the text more relevant or more meaningful to an audience. This may involve "modernizing" an older text (for example, setting *Canterbury Tales* on a bus to the cathedral), or it may mean that you change the format of the text (such as transforming the opening scenes of *The Scarlet Letter* into a script for a dramatic version of the story). In either case, you will be graded on your originality, creativity, and grammatical skills.

1. Begin by selecting a section of the text to revise. The section you choose should be easy to work with and include some significant action within the story. As a guideline, you should plan to revise a full act of a play or a full chapter of a novel, producing a work of your own of roughly the same length (number of pages or scenes). Be sure to have your selection approved before you begin. Your teacher will tell you if you've chosen an appropriate section of the text and warn you if you're taking on too much.
2. Once you've chosen your material, begin revising. A few key points to keep in mind:

   a. Be consistent. Don't modernize part of a story and leave dialogue in its original form elsewhere. If you move a Shakespearean play into the twentieth century, don't include language from the Renaissance period unless absolutely necessary. State leaders these days rarely say things such as "A pox on both your houses!"
   b. Avoid anachronisms. Again, if you modernize a story, modernize the *whole* story. How likely are you to find twentieth-century characters fighting with swords? Pardoners may have been around in Chaucer's time, but the church doesn't sell pardons today. What would a pardoner be doing for a living today?
   c. Remember the advantages of your format. If you're converting a play to a novel, take advantage of the novel's use of interior monologue to give us insights into character motivations or attitudes an actor would have conveyed

through motions or expressions on stage. If you're going from novel to play, take advantage of the drama's use of monologue to share character motivations. Don't be afraid to change lines, as long as you remain within the general plot outline of the story.

3. After writing your first draft, show it to a peer or your teacher and ask for comments. Revise your draft as needed, addressing any weaknesses or missing plot elements your reader points out.

4. Carefully polish your final version. Proofread it to catch any spelling errors you may have made and any grammatical problems that may have slipped by. Reading your work out loud at this point can help you identify problem sentences quickly and spot misspelling. Once you are certain that you've edited out any problems, turn in the assignment to your teacher. Your work may be read or performed before the class if time permits and it is of high quality.

Staged Performance

In this assignment, you and your peers will select a scene from the novel or play you've been reading and present a live performance of that scene to the class. You will be expected to memorize your lines and stage the action appropriately, and costuming and props are recommended. You should perform a scene important to the story. Don't choose a scene in which some minor plot development occurs.

1. Select your scene. Your choice should be based on the importance of the scene to the text as a whole. Does it contain key developments in the story? Does it involve major characters? Is it a climactic moment? The more dramatic the section you choose, the more impact it will have when you perform it. As a rule, each actor in your group should have a minimum of twenty lines to memorize; one actor may play two characters who aren't on stage simultaneously. Your teacher must approve choice of scene, so have it checked *before* you start memorizing lines.

2. Plan your performance. Read over the scene as a group, making sure that everyone understands what is being said by their characters and what the action of the scene is. If you don't know what your character is saying or doing, how will you know how to behave on stage? Once everyone is clear on the dialogue and action, begin blocking your scene. Blocking is the process of deciding where people will stand during the scene and how they will move about. There are two major rules for blocking to follow:

   • An actor should never stand between another actor and the audience. "Upstaging" keeps the audience from seeing the whole drama.
   • Actors should never turn their backs on the audience. Lines delivered while an actor faces the back of the stage are almost impossible to hear, and the audience won't be able to see your facial expressions.

3. Rehearse early and often. If you don't practice, you won't know what to do if your partner forgets lines. You'll also be too distracted by the effort of remembering

your lines to actually act the part. Rehearsals can also help you catch problems with your blocking or props before the graded performance.

4. Choose costumes and props. Having each actor be responsible for outfitting his or her own character is often the best way, but you may have one person handle all the costumes and another obtain the props.

5. Perform your scene for the class. Your performance will be graded on accuracy, creative effort, and quality of performance. Accuracy is measured by how many lines you remembered and whether you recited them correctly. Creative effort shows in costuming, props, and staging. Although you will not be judged like full-time actors or even drama students, your score on performance quality will be based on your acting efforts—how well you use your voice, facial expressions, and body language to convey the emotions your character is feeling.

Videotaped Performance

In this assignment, you and your peers will select a scene from the novel or play you've been reading and videotape a performance of that scene to play for the class. You will be expected to memorize your lines and stage the action appropriately, and costuming and props are recommended. Perform a scene important to the story rather than a scene in which some minor plot development occurs.

1. Select your scene. Your choice should be based on the importance of the scene to the text as a whole. Does it contain key developments in the story? Does it involve major characters? Is it a climactic moment? The more dramatic the section you choose, the more impact it will have when you perform it. As a rule, each actor in your group should have a minimum of twenty lines to memorize; one actor may play two characters who aren't on stage simultaneously. Because your choice of scene must be approved by the teacher, have it checked *before* you start memorizing lines.

2. Plan your performance. You'll need to make arrangements with your school's media center or broadcasting department to borrow a videotape recorder, and you'll need a blank tape or two for recording. You'll probably want to determine when your group can get together for filming before you check out the recorder. Decide where you'll film and when.

3. Read over the scene as a group, making sure that everyone understands what is being said by their characters and what the action of the scene is. If you don't know what your character is saying or doing, how will you know how to behave on stage? Once everyone is clear on the dialogue and action, begin blocking your scene. Blocking is the process of deciding where people will stand during the scene and how they will move about. There are two major rules for blocking to follow:

   • An actor should never stand between another actor and the audience. "Upstaging" keeps the audience from seeing the whole drama.
   • Actors should never turn their backs on the audience. Lines you deliver while facing the back of the stage are almost impossible to hear, and the audience won't be able to see your facial expressions.

4. Rehearse early and often. If you don't practice, you won't know what to do if your partner forgets lines. You'll also be too distracted by the effort of remembering your lines to actually act the part. Rehearsals can also help you catch problems with your blocking or props before you tape.

5. Choose costumes and props. Having each actor be responsible for outfitting his or her own character is often the best way, but you may have one person handle all the costumes and another obtain the props.

6. Videotape your scene. Your performance will be graded on accuracy, creative effort, and quality of performance. Accuracy is measured by how many lines you remembered and whether you recited them correctly. Creative effort shows in costuming, props, and staging, as well as in the clarity of the sound on your tape and the quality of the video work. If you can't be clearly seen or heard, you won't receive full credit for your performance. Although you will not be judged like full-time actors or even drama students, your score on performance quality will be based on your acting efforts—how well you use your voice and your facial expressions to convey the emotions your character is feeling. Because videotaping is difficult to master and sound quality often varies on a videotape, you may wish to film your scene twice to give yourself two versions to choose from when you turn in your work.

7. Review your tape before turning it in. Is it your best work? Did everyone perform well? Were the lines clearly delivered and audible? Can you see everyone and everything the audience is supposed to see? If something didn't go well, consider taping the scene again before submitting it for your group's final grade.

Set Design

In this assignment, you will produce complete set designs for the play you are studying. These designs will show important features such as entrances, exits, and set pieces for each scene of the play in question and include drawings of each major scene from the audience's point of view. Drawings should be on paper the size of an art pad, not on letter- or legal-size paper. Set designs should be on graph paper.

1. Begin by reviewing the play and making a list of sets required. A set change is required when the action moves from one location to another or when a major event changes the existing set in some way (furniture is moved around, extended time passes between scenes, etc.). Your play may have many set changes, or it may have only one or two.

2. Using a piece of graph paper, lay out the first set used in the play. Remember that you may not get much description in the stage directions, and you'll have to reread the scene to make sure you have all the furniture mentioned on your design. You may add more furniture (set pieces) to the set if you like, but be careful not to add so much that you begin to obstruct the movement of the characters. Try to maintain a realistic size balance in your graph. Make each square one

or two feet, and use a suitable number of squares to represent each set piece. Be sure to include entrances and exits to the set.

3. Draw a picture of the set as it would be seen from the audience. Include the proscenium arch and curtains, if visible. Remember to include any props that would be on tables, sofas, desks, and other furniture at the beginning of the scene. This picture does not have to be artist quality, but you should have clearly spent time working on the project.

4. Repeat the process for the next set change.

5. Note that you will be graded on the quality and accuracy of your designs as well as your creativity. Allowances will be made for artistic skills, but bear in mind that you have other options for completing this ring. If you choose this project, your drawings will be held to reasonably high standards. The number of scene changes you need to design will also affect the standard you are held to. If you have only one or two changes to design, your drawings and designs should show a great deal of time and effort; if you have seven or eight changes, less detail is acceptable.

Soundtrack

In this assignment, you will produce a soundtrack for the novel or play you are working with. You will write "liner notes" for your work to explain why you chose each selection in your compilation. Finally, you will design a graphic for your tape case. This assignment requires a sixty-minute cassette tape and access to recording equipment.

1. Make a list of the events in the novel or play. This chronology should include all the major events in the story; remember that the more events you list, the more choices you'll have to draw on for your soundtrack.

2. Once you've finished your list, begin to narrow it down. You'll have sixty minutes to work with, so you can plan on using seven or eight songs per side of the tape, for a total of fourteen to sixteen entries.

3. Choose your songs. Your choices should illustrate or enhance the event they are associated with. For each choice, write at least a paragraph on why you chose that music. What makes it appropriate for the moment?

4. Record your soundtrack. After you have completed your recording, be sure to play back the tape to check that the recording is clear.

5. Create the case. You may cut and paste pictures from clip art sources, the Internet, and magazines, or you may decide to take your own picture for the cover. If you prefer, you can create a CD jewel case instead of a tape case; jewel cases can be purchased at any music store for $1.99 or so.

6. Turn in your completed tape, along with the tape or jewel case and the liner notes. If time permits, you may be allowed to present your case and play a song for the class.

Comic Book

In this assignment, you will create a comic book version of a portion of the novel or play you have been studying. In the process of creating the comic book, you may need to rewrite some of the dialogue; if you are working with a novel, you will almost certainly need to distill the text to essential moments. This assignment will be graded on the basis of creativity and accuracy. Because it requires extensive drawing, it should be undertaken only by students who are confident of their art skills. A variety of pencils and pens and a supply of art paper will be needed for this assignment.

1. Begin by deciding which portion of the text you will be drawing. In a play, an act is a good length. With a novel, look for a section in which a major plot development takes place, preferably one involving action. You may want to check with your teacher to see if your choice seems appropriate.
2. Outline the plot events for yourself on paper to create a "storyboard," your guide for the action in your comic book. This is a good time to cut down to the essential details of your story.
3. Next, begin sketching your comic. Rough out drawings so that you know what will be happening in each panel; divide your pages into no more than five panels and no fewer than two. Remember to leave room for dialogue.
4. Draw your final versions of each panel, beginning with pencil; then ink each panel to make the lines neat and clear. You don't need to color your drawings, but you may.
5. Your comic should have a cover page to protect it, but you do not need to create a special drawing for the cover.
6. Your finished comic should be at least five pages in length, although longer work is certainly acceptable. Remember, you will be graded on the quality of your artwork and the care you take with your adaptation, so think carefully about choosing this project.

Ring Three Assignment Guidelines

Analytical Assignments

Compare or Contrast Essay

In this assignment, you will demonstrate your comprehension of the text you have been studying by comparing or contrasting it with another novel, play, or movie. This is a formal writing assignment requiring a thesis, analysis of evidence, and conclusions presented with proper citations and MLA formatting. Your essay will be graded for both content and grammar, and it should be three to five pages long, typed, and double-spaced.

1. Develop a thesis. Your thesis should include not only a statement about the similarities or differences in the two works but also an explanation of why those simi-

larities or differences are important. What do we learn from your comparison, and why is it important? Remember that this is a compare *or* contrast essay. You may not do both in a single paper. Attempting to focus on both similarities and differences often produces two sets of examples that cancel each other out, leaving no conclusion for the reader. Although you may need to acknowledge some similarities in a contrast essay or some differences in a comparison essay, your primary objective is to prove that the two works are similar or that they are different.

2. Outline your essay. On a separate sheet of paper, outline at least three points you will make to prove your thesis, and make sure you have at least one example in each work for each point. This means that you will use a minimum of six examples for your paper.

3. Write your first draft. Concentrate on getting across the points you intend to make to your reader in a convincing manner. Avoid plot summary. Tell your readers only what they absolutely need to know to understand your essay. When you've finished, submit the essay to your teacher for comments.

4. Revise the essay based on your teacher's comments. Be sure to answer any questions he or she presents; simply cleaning up the grammar and punctuation and ignoring the content-related issues raised will hurt your final grade.

5. Submit a clean, spell-checked copy of your final draft to your teacher, with your first draft attached.

Scene Presentation or Interpretation

In this assignment, you will demonstrate your comprehension of the text you have been studying by twice acting out a scene from it for the class. By altering the movement, appearance, facial expressions, or vocal tone of the characters, you will present two different interpretations of a single scene to demonstrate the possibilities a director has in performing a text. This assignment may be undertaken alone or with a group of two or three other students. This assignment works best with a play, but you may choose to do a dramatic presentation of a novel or a poem, which may require some adaptation of the original text.

1. Choose your scene. Although your choice may be influenced by the number of people in your group, it should be primarily based on your ability to interpret the scene in a variety of ways. Scenes in which a character's reaction to events is not clearly written into the stage directions are ideal for this assignment. For example, students studying *Macbeth* might want to consider how Macbeth would deliver his lines. Is he loud and overbearing, foolishly tempted by the witches, or does he speak quietly and deliberately, with cunning in his tone? How old is he, and how would that affect the way his character is presented in each scene? Is Lady Macbeth gently persuasive, or is she so dominant in her marriage that her husband dares not contradict her? Such choices can change the viewer's opinion of a character and his or her behavior.

2. Study your part. Each actor should learn his or her lines for the scene, and the group should meet to practice the scene before performing for the class. This

assignment requires attention to details like tone and movement that are difficult if you have not memorized the lines in advance.

3. Block the scenes. Decide how and when people will move, speak, and act during each version of the scene. You may decide to divide the workload. Designate one member of your group to be in charge of where people will stand and move, another to obtain props, a third to set up the stage for performance, and so on. You will be graded on both the creativity of your presentations and the clarity of the difference in the two versions of the scene, so plan carefully.

4. Perform your scene for the class. Before you begin each version of the scene, you may wish to explain to the audience what you will be changing about each character and what that change means to our opinion of that character.

5. Each actor is also required to turn in a one-page explanation of how their character was altered from one version to the other and what that alteration would do to a viewer's opinion of the character. These short responses are due at the time of your presentation.

Character Analysis Essay (Kiersey Temperament Sorter)

In this assignment, you will choose a character from the play, novel, or poem you are studying and write a character profile and analysis for that person. You will first use an online test to identify the personality type and traits associated with the character and then discuss in an essay the appropriateness of the test results. This assignment requires access to the World Wide Web.

1. Using a Web browser such as Netscape Navigator or Microsoft Internet Explorer, access the World Wide Web. In the navigation window at the top of the browser, type the URL <http://www.kiersey.com> and press Go or Enter. You should find yourself at the Kiersey Temperament Sorter Web site. Scrolling down if necessary, find the link to Kiersey Temperament Sorter II and click it. You should find yourself at the beginning of a questionnaire.

2. Choose the character you plan to discuss and begin taking the test *as if you were that character.* For example, a question may be, "Which would you rather do on Saturday night?" and offer "Stay home and watch a rented movie" or "Go to the most popular nightclub in town" as possible answers. Choose the answer that you believe the character would select, even if it isn't the answer you yourself would give. You may need to think carefully about some of the questions. Deciding whether Grendel, from *Beowulf,* is the sort of monster who would answer his phone at once or if he'd rather let it ring may seem hard, but rethinking the question (asking, instead, if he prefers to talk to others or to be left alone, for example) may make it easier to answer.

3. When you complete the test, write down the results you are given for your character's temperament and variant temperament, as well as the letters and numbers labeled "details of questionnaire." After recording this information, click on the link for your character's variant temperament to read more about traits and behavior associated with this personality type.

4. Decide whether your character matches up well with the assigned personality type. Then, in an essay, argue why the test was or was not accurate for your character, using specific examples from the text to point out behavior associated with the assigned personality type or behavior that is inappropriate for that personality type. Focus your attention on the characteristics with particularly high scores in the "details" section. For example, your test may have resulted in Grendel receiving a score of +16 in the I (introspective/internal) category and a +2 in the J (judging) category. These scores indicate that Grendel's behavior should strongly reflect an introspective nature but that the judging side of his personality is not nearly so consistent. In general, higher scores (particularly scores of 10 or more) in an area suggest that that area will be frequently reflected in the person's behavior pattern.

5. Conclude your essay by discussing why your results may have come out the way they did. If the character was identified, for example, as a Guardian/Protector type, what about the character's role in the story might have suggested that type of personality? If the results seem out-of-line with the character's behavior in the story, what might have produced the confusion? Would the character have been more believable in the story if he or she had been given a personality that matched the profile?

You may wish to explore the Kiersey Sorter Web site for more information on the sorter, its accuracy and value, and the various personality types.

INDEXES

Author Index

Time Period Index

Plays with "Red Flags"

Plays without "Red Flags"